It's Only Hell If You Make It That Way

Surviving in Federal Prison

G V Profeta

Order this book online at www.trafford.com
or email orders@trafford.com

Most Trafford titles are also available at major online book retailers.

Printed in the United States of America.

ISBN: 978-1-4907-2361-7 (sc)
ISBN: 978-1-4907-2362-4 (hc)
ISBN: 978-1-4907-2363-1 (e)

Library of Congress Control Number: 2014900520

Trafford rev.   04/23/2014

 www.trafford.com

North America & international
toll-free: 1 888 232 4444 (USA & Canada)
fax: 812 355 4082

Contents

Author's Note

I was released from federal prison in early Spring of 2010, after serving fifty-three months of a sixty-one-month sentence. You *must* realize that if you are going to prison in the Fed, your sentence is going to be considerably longer than if you were going to do state time for the same offense. In many instances, you may not even do time with a state charge, but instead, just be put on probation and be required to do community service. While the state sentences for like offenses may be less, the conditions in a state prison compared to federal prisons are, in many cases, worse. At least be thankful that you will be going to a prison system where you will less likely be injured or have to put up with very poor living conditions. I am not saying you will be immune to those issues I just mentioned, but the conditions in the state system are more conducive to a rougher time for first-time offenders.

There are many books in circulation that talk about prison life, and many of the authors take an amusing or comical approach in those works. The sad thing about prison life is that there is nothing funny about it. Actually, one can say that the federal system in and of itself is a joke, but that is a story for another book. In this book I tell it "like it is." You will notice that the institution you will be going to will sugarcoat the facility whenever some kind of regional or federal inspection is due, but I do not sugarcoat anything in this book. I am going to relate to you every pertinent aspect of prison life, be it good or bad. It will be up to you how you process this information and put it to use.

Most of you reading this book, who look at incarceration, will be spending time in more than one institution unless your sentence is under five years. Most federal sentences are over five years, so it is safe to say that you will be bounced around a little bit. In my case, I spent equal time (eighteen months at two institutions) and now am safely home and employed—a huge plus.

Before heading to prison, I spent eighteen months in a county jail that had a federal holdover pod while awaiting the outcome of my case. Once sentenced, I was transferred to the federal satellite low at Jesup, Georgia, where I spent the first half of the remainder of my sentence. In December of 2008, I was moved to Miami FCI (the original Club Fed) and was there until my release. Most of this book was written while I was at Jesup FSL, but within a month of being in Miami, I noticed that there was a huge difference in how the two facilities operate. Compared to Miami, Jesup FSL, to me, is what one would call rinky-dink. It is a much-laid-back facility, and the administration there does nothing to promote any type of inmate initiatives. On the other hand, at Miami, the staff there, especially in the Education and Psychology Departments, do what they can to help the inmate gear himself for life beyond the razor wire. Jesup cut out their computer courses, as well as woodworking and other craft-type classes. Jesup has no career training center, and the staff is undertrained and ineffectual. In my first month at Miami FCI, I had already begun taking an international trading course and started on Computer Applications I. I took the keyboarding class and passed and can now type close to forty-one words per minute. I had started Rosetta Stone Spanish but was released a short way into the classes. I thought that Jesup was the place to do your time but soon realized that if you want to further your education and be better prepared for reentering society, then Jesup is not where you want to go. Yes, Jesup has open dorms where inmates live in cubicle-type cells with no doors, and that seems to be the only plus. At Miami, you are locked in your cells even though it is classified as a low, and it took getting used to being trapped like an animal again. In Miami though, I found that one can better prepare himself for public life a lot easier than one can at Jesup. What I have heard from other inmates, most facilities are like Miami, where you can work on getting ready for a new life after prison. These are just two examples of federal prisons located throughout the country. In the end, it will be up to you on how you do your time. There is nothing wrong or unmacho about wanting to better yourself. Prison is definitely not fun, but it is not the end of the world either.

Acknowledgments

First and foremost, I must thank my brother for his unending love and support from day 1 in December of 2005 up until the day I walked out of prison in the Spring of 2010. Thank you, bro, for keeping me in commissary for my time in prison as well as paying for the storage of my property. Thanks for paying my legal fees during the divorce I wish never happened, as well as acting as power of attorney for all the other legal matters that needed taking care of.

If not for you and your unselfish generosity, giving up of your time to come see me and be at my court appearances, and for your financial support, you probably would have had to pay for my funeral too.

Thanks also go out to your wonderful wife, my sister-in-law, for all that you have done for me right before my release and shortly after, when I needed transportation and moral support while holding over in Decatur while waiting to get back home.

I do not know what kind of shape I would be in if it were not for my two dearest friends of the past five years, let alone the past forty years.

OB, thank you for being there every time I called you at work and for being the same old friend that I grew up with since high school. Your letters and e-mails kept me laughing and wanting to throw on some camouflage and head for the woods to do some hunting.

Your faith in God and encouragement helped me to remain positive and want to have the whole ordeal get over with real soon.

Thank your assistant for me, for it was nice to hear another kind voice on the phone when you were out of the studio.

Beachy, what can I say? Yeah, yeah, yeah—I should have rented a video. Better words couldn't be spoken, and when you told me that in our first phone call, you actually got me to laugh. Something I had not done since being arrested. Hearing your voice on the phone and reading your letters and e-mails have assured me that I am still loved by some people.

Your steadfast faith in God has rubbed off on me, and I am a better Christian, as well as a better human being, thanks to you. The scripture that you sent to me that you as well told me to read on a daily basis has helped me to develop a closer relationship with Christ and, in turn, has brought me closer to my son. (I must also thank Dr. Craig for keeping my head in the Bible throughout my ordeal.)

Beachy, we have both experienced some pretty bad times over the past few years, and our faith, as well as our friendship, seems to have gotten us through the hard parts. I look forward to sharing a nice glass of red with you when we get together, and maybe, we can find something to laugh about with regard to our individual prisons that we had to endure during the late '00s.

Number 5 and your wonderful wife, thank you for believing in me and coming to my aid when I asked for your help. I deeply regret that I did not come through and repay you when you needed the funds and feel like such an idiot for letting you two down. When I needed your help, like addicts do, I lied to you. I can only ask for your forgiveness, and while I cannot make you forgive me, I can only ask God that he allow us to one day sit back and enjoy the memories of Martha, George, and Mr. B. I actually ran into a few of the boys that knew Mr. B., Streaky, and Martha's gang while at Miami FCI.

Mike P., thanks for remaining my friend and for letting me know how to take my head out of my ass. I deserved your tough comments, and you can punch me when we see each other again and tell me what an asshole I was.

Finally, I want to thank my ex-wife and my children.

I will start with my son, seeing as we have once again gotten back together, which started late in my stay at Jesup and has continued now that I am home.

Your e-mails in 2008 and 2009 lifted my life and my spirits to new heights once I realized you always were willing to communicate with me but found it hard to write. Thank God for e-mail.

Coming back into my life at the time you did helped me fight off the depression that was taking my life slowly from me. Your communications lit up my life and helped me get back to the good me I used to be. We have a lot of catching up to do, and I look forward to getting you out on the golf course so that I can kick your butt.

At publication time, I can sadly announce that I have yet to communicate with my daughter and have not heard from her in almost eight years. I feed off the wonderful memories we shared as dad and daughter and always can picture her vividly doing the crazy things she did as a kid. Our times together greatly outweigh the bad that I had caused with my arrest and imprisonment. My daughter has disenfranchised me as a parent, and I do not blame her for being mad at me, seeing all the pain and embarrassment I caused her. I ask God every day to give me my daughter back. I will never stop loving you and look forward to the day when I can hold you in my arms and tell you I love you in person.

Even though we are divorced after twenty-one years of marriage, I want to thank my ex-wife for having the patience and fortitude to put up with "three children" over all those years before my arrest. After spending the last eighteen months of my imprisonment picking up after a cell mate that was as childish as I was when I was living at home, I now see clearly why you fell out of love with me and slept in the family room. I never grew up, and I failed you as a husband and, in some ways, failed our children as a father.

It really sucks that it took me having to go to prison to find out what a lousy person I was to live with. While I may have thought I was a good person by doing good things in the community, I was not doing good things at home. Maybe someday, you too can forgive me for being such an ass.

Your constant updates and letters kept me informed as to how our children were doing, as well as my friends and siblings. Those updates were invaluable for they were my only real connection with the outside world.

I am so glad that you are doing well in your profession and wish you the best.

I still miss my family, many friends, and all my relatives and hope to see many of you soon. One does not realize how much people mean to you until you are no longer with them. Everyone I did not mention that stood by me, I thank you for remaining my friend and not judging me as many have done. God bless all of you.

Prison really sucked!

Introduction

You (or someone that you know and/or care about) are going to prison, and there is nothing one can do about it. You may be going away for six months, six years, or for life—it does not matter; you are still going to a place that will put everything that you have learned on the outside to the test on the inside. Some will make it through their tenure behind the razor wire without even so much as a scratch while others may not be as fortunate.

I did my time and was down for over four years and have seen how things work. I have seen that it does not matter how big and how mean you are (though that does have its advantages) but, instead, how smart you are with regard to making your life safe and secure.

You will be entering a culture totally different from the one you have grown accustomed to on the outside. You will need to adapt, or your time in prison will drag on and you will have nothing but problems. You will need to be a patient individual and will also need to leave your ego in the real world somewhere. You can always go back to it when you get out.

You will be going to a place where the "animals run the zoo." While there may be administrators and corrections officers on the compound at all times, it is the inmates that dictate how things are done. In prison, it is the black inmates that control everything, from who watches TV and where to what items are sold in the commissary each month. Unlike outside the walls, whites are the minority while black inmates make up the majority. If you happen to be white, sit back and do your time. Do not try to change things, because you will be putting a target on your chest without even realizing it until it is too late. If you are black, take comfort in the fact that your life will be easier than that of most of the other ethnic groups that make up your prison population. If you are Hispanic, European, Chinese, Korean, or whatever, you too make up a portion of the minority and should try to make it through your sentence without making trouble for yourself. There are prisons with a large Mexican or Hispanic population, and these groups sometimes compete right up there with the blacks for control of who runs the show. So if you are white, just sit back and enjoy the show, and if you are black, good luck being the boss.

While prison is a sad and bad place, it will definitely be an education. You will be able to take some of what you learned in prison back to the streets, but for the most case, you will want to leave it all behind.

Prison life is a way of surviving and nothing more. Do not think you will be rehabilitated, because that method had disappeared somewhere in the sixties. Prison in the 2000s is nothing but one huge time-out, just one elongated punishment. The choice is up to you if you want to leave prison a better person. Men and women who come to prison as "good people" will most likely leave as good people, but men and women who come to prison as "bad people," in most instances, leave worse than when they had arrived. That is the reason I am writing this book: so that people who have never been to prison before can pick out the good inmates from the bad and learn what is necessary to remain "good."

I have put together this book to help you get through your prison life with as little trouble as possible. A lot will depend on how you carry yourself. You will be able to use this book as a guide. Either you can do your time without being noticed or you can draw attention to yourself, thus making your time behind the razor wire the most dreaded time of your life. You do not want to go through your time in prison always having to look over your shoulder, because sooner or later, you will look too late and you will be hit with whatever your enemy can find to harm you with, and most of the time, it is not his fist. It is too bad we all cannot be like our mothers used to be. Remember when growing up, all our moms had eyes behind their heads. If we were like our moms, life in prison would be much easier. But we are not, so I am going to tell you how you can make your tenure a little easier and less stressful. I have found that it is much simpler to use your brain before resorting to any other means, and when one does use his intellect to survive, it makes it harder for others to figure you out, and that is what you want. In prison, it is the men and women who cannot be figured out who are left alone. That is what you want to do if you plan on making it through your campaign in one piece and with peace of mind.

The best advice I can give any of you going away for the first time is, make the others hate your charges and not the person. If you can do that, you will see that life won't be that bad. This book will not help you if you make inmates hate you. You will be on your own, and as the Terminator once said, "Hasta la vista, baby."

I have listed the ways (mostly legal and some not so legal) in which you can safely maneuver your way through prison. There are a few ways that are not exactly prison policy, but because most corrections officers (COs) tend to look the other way, you may find yourself running or using these services as well. It is just how things are; I am not going to lie. In every federal institution, you will be able to find the COs, staff, or administrators that are "on the take" and use this knowledge to your advantage. Things have been going on like this way before you or I have arrived in prison and will keep on going that way long after we leave. Like I mentioned in the Author's Note, nothing is sugarcoated, and I think that I have done a good job showing you this in my book. Prison is tough, let's face it. Either you can make it even tougher or you can make it a little easier—it is totally up to you.

I hope that this book will help you make your decisions and your life behind the razor wire a little bit more bearable.

MISTAKE versus BAD CHOICE

Before I get into the meat and potatoes of you going to prison and how you should act in order to survive and get out someday in one piece and be a better person, I must say this: what you did to get yourself into this predicament was not by mistake but instead by a bad choice that you made. What everyone says, "We all make mistakes, you just got caught," is so untrue in many instances. You made a conscious decision to do what you did and ultimately got arrested. Misspelling a word is a mistake, or thinking someone is someone else is a mistake. Robbing a bank, selling drugs, driving drunk, sexually abusing someone, killing someone, or whatever crime you committed is the result of a choice that you made. Somewhere in your life, be it recently or many years ago, you allowed yourself or your brain to develop bad choices as the only way for you to go forward in your decision-making process. This risk-taking behavior could have been the result of poor family life and relationships; being abused mentally, sexually, or physically at some time in your past; or any other number of experiences or life-changing events that affect the way you think. I am not a psychologist, social worker, or a professional in the field of study of behaviors, but I am one who has gone down the same dark path you have and am just finishing up my third year of therapy where I am trying to find out when and why my brain short-circuited to the point where I allowed bad decisions to be the norm and not the exception as part of my daily behavior and decision making.

SEEMINGLY UNIMPORTANT DECISIONS (SUD)

From June 2010 until May 2013 (and possibly further), I was seeing Larry Auerbach, LCSW (licensed certified social worker), BCETS (board-certified expert in traumatic stress). Mr. Auerbach made it known to me and my group that every day we make decisions that determine the outcome of our life, be these decisions good or bad, thus making the results of these decisions good or bad as well. He has instilled or at least tried to instill in all of us attending how important it is to think through every decision we have to make where we see risk involved. Sometimes, the risk is not dangerous or criminal, but on many occasions, the risks we may involve ourselves in have negative consequences. It is during these risk-taking, decision-making times that we have to look at the possible results and make our decision according to that outcome result. People like me and you, the reader of this book, evidently overlooked the possible consequences of the risk-taking behavior we were allowing ourselves to partake in and went ahead and made a decision that not only had negative consequences but ones that could have been extremely dangerous as well. We ignored all the warnings and made a bad choice. This harmful behavior was the result of a seemingly unimportant decision or an SUD. Mr. Auerbach describes an SUD as the following:

What is a seemingly unimportant decision, and why is it a strong warning of a dangerous situation? The best way to define an SUD is to say that it is the first step on a banana peel that can lead to a slip and then a fall that could create a prolonged stay in a hospital or even a wheelchair or, at the very worse, lead to death. It is the conscious choice to not see a potential risk or danger that can often lead to a bigger risk and danger and a situation that an individual cannot escape from without risking a great loss or injury, either physically, financially, emotionally, or any combination of these.

There are certain phrases that are used by the individual who is making this SUD that if they really listened to themselves, would tell them that they are on the verge of making this poorly-thought-out and dangerous choice. Some of these common warning phrases are "It's only . . ." "I'm just . . ." "It's not really . . ." "Everyone does this . . ." "I know I shouldn't do/say this, but . . ." and "It can't hurt if I . . ." Anytime someone hears themselves saying these things, it would be a very good idea to pay close attention to the words that follow and think about the possible consequences that may occur if they go ahead with their plans. But this is the underlying problem with someone making an SUD—they are most often choosing to not see the potential disaster this choice can bring into their lives because their focus is on what the gain could be. The desire to see only the rewards blinds them to the possibility that there are pitfalls or problems with the behavior they are thinking of engaging in. It is the first step of a mistake in judgment that usually leads to a series of successive mistakes that only serve to compound the problem, increasing the danger at each turn, and leading the individual deeper into trouble at each decision. Because the individual is only looking at the desired end result, they will often miss the warning signs at each step of the process, blindly following their *desire into a pit that they will seldom be able to climb out of unscathed or without a significant cost to themselves.*

By focusing on what one wants to see instead of what is truly there, anyone can put themselves in the position of making a seemingly unimportant decision that can forever change their life and the lives of others in ways that can never be undone or repaired.

To put it simply, look before you leap.

Now, for the meat and potatoes.

YOU ARE GOING TO PRISON

If you bought this book, more than likely, you are looking at going to prison in the near future. No, not because you purchased the book, but because your actions have dictated that law enforcement arrest you, charge you, and have you locked up.

By now, you already know if you are going to prison or not. You will have either made bail and will have to self-surrender on an appointed date, or you will remain in custody and will be designated to a prison and then transferred there at the BOP's discretion. If you are going to self-surrender, you do not need to read this chapter. If you are remanded or decide to remain in custody, it will benefit you to read on.

OK, you did not make bond and have to begin serving your sentence from the day you were arrested. In a way, this is a good thing because your sentence has already begun being counted down even if you have not been sentenced yet.

For every day that you are locked up, you are accruing good time, no matter where you are, be it a federal holdover, a local or county jail, or anywhere that the BOP has you in custody. In my case, I remained at a county jail, in its federal "pod," for over sixteen months while my counsel was working on getting me the best "deal" they could with the prosecution. The bad thing was that I actually did get awarded bond and could have gone home, but for personal reasons, that was not going to happen, so I remained in custody. While I would have loved to be out among family and friends, getting my affairs in order, I think that I would really have wanted to put in as much time as I could up front so that this nightmare would be behind me as quickly as I could get it there. By remaining in custody, I cut off eighteen months that would have had to be added on once I self-surrendered. I look back now and thank God I did not go home on bond. Some people call me crazy, but if I did go home, I would be in prison until almost 2012. No way.

If you are in custody, then you are somewhat familiar with how the facility you are in works. In most instances, it is nothing like being in a federal prison, and in nine out of ten cases, you will find it much better in the Fed once you get there. Being locked up for a month to many months will prove invaluable, and it is best that you do your time there without making yourself a target. The less you interact with people, the better you will be. I am not saying you do not speak to anyone, but when you do, choose your acquaintances wisely and keep the number low. You will be able to tell the good "eggs" from the bad. Stay away from the bad as much as you can. Another thing to remember while you are in prison is that there is no social order among inmates. If you were the CEO of your company or some homeless person on the street, it will not mean a thing in prison. If you are used to getting your way on the outside, forget it, and I mean forget it. Once you start to make a fuss about all the little things that are not right, you will be asking for trouble. Suck it up and go with the flow the best that you can. It will be very difficult at first, but prison is unlike anywhere you have been before.

However long you are in a preprison lockup, you will come across some similarities with how things operate in the Fed. Depending on your security classification, your housing will be a big part of how well one adjusts to being locked up. More than likely, you are in a cell with one or possibly more cell mates. This cell is most likely locked every evening at lights-out and whenever your facility has a "standing count," which in most cases is at 4:00 p.m. You learn quickly how to use the toilet and other facilities in your cell and do it so that no one else in your cell is offended or made to clean up after you. The one constant of being in a holding facility is that you will be locked up. This also goes for being in a medium-security prison and higher. Most lows, satellite lows, and camps do not have cells, but instead, you will be living in dormitory-like settings, and you will be assigned to a cubicle-type cell. No doors, no toilets in your room, just you, your cell mates, lockers, and a desk with a chair for each celly. You have a little more freedom, and it really feels good not being closed in a cage every night. If you can survive the lockup you are in now, it won't get any worse unless you are going to a maximum-security prison.

While at holdover facilities, you will be allowed certain privileges and have some amenities that are similar to those in the prison you will be going to in the near future. Here are some of those features that you will use on a daily and weekly basis.

COMMISSARY. You will be allowed to purchase food and sundry items once a week. This will free you up from having to eat the meals prepared daily for the inmates or at least supplement them. It also gives you a little freedom in choosing better items for hygiene, such as soaps, shampoos, and deodorants. The list you choose from will not be as extensive as at a federal prison, but you will get a good idea how the system works. You will also learn how to have funds put into your inmate account. Be sure that when you are finally designated to a prison, your money follows you. Some holdovers have their own inmate accounts, and they are not the same as the lockbox fund used by the Feds. If they have their own accounts, your money may not be transferred to the facility you are sent to right away. Be patient; it usually shows up within one week.

LAUNDRY. Most likely, you will be issued two or three jumpsuits and a few pairs of briefs, T-shirts, and socks. Each week, you are required to turn in your soiled laundry to be washed and returned the same day. The same goes for bed linens.

RECREATION. Depending on the holdover that you are at, recreation can be anything from being allowed out a cement yard surrounded by walls and razor wire to being allowed into a gym where there a few things to do, such as play basketball, walk, play Ping-Pong, or sit down and play board games. Consider yourself lucky if you get to go to rec once a week. In many instances, men and women don't go to rec but for once or twice a month. When you are allowed rec, it is usually for about one hour. These change drastically for the good when you get to your prison.

LIBRARIES AND EDUCATION. Forget about wanting to take any kind of classes at a holdover or going to the library to read. These facilities do not offer either. Holdovers have computers for law work and tiny book carts that rarely make it to the different pods for inmates to choose books off of. The majority of books on the book carts usually are made up of bibles and other religious books. The best way to do some reading is to have family send books to you.

VISITS. You will be allowed visits, but you will have to speak to your friends and loved ones through the use of a phone while viewing them through a plexiglass barrier.

MEALS. I won't go into meals, seeing as the meals served in the Fed are much better than the meals you are being served now.

For most of you reading this, you have been in a holdover facility for a little while and are familiar with its workings. If you are waiting to go to your designated prison, let the "fun" begin.

TRANSFERRED . . . FINALLY!

Your case has been settled, and your lawyer tells you that you have been designated to a prison. No one knows where you are going or when, but figure sometime within the next forty-five days. For security reasons, nobody can tell you where or when. Most holdovers will not allow inmates to take certain foods and sundry items with them to prison, so order commissary carefully. You will be informed by a CO to pack all your personal property that you want to take with you and what you want picked up or sent home. When that happens, figure that you will be leaving within the week and, usually, in a day or two.

Now is when the real "fun" begins—again. You will be pulled out of your unit/cell early in the morning, usually before 3:00 a.m. You will be processed out; issued bus clothes; and handcuffed, chained, and shackled for the umpteenth time. Depending on what part of the country you are going, you will be driven to a federal holdover or transfer center. In my case, I was bussed to the Atlanta USP, then off to Tallahassee FDC, and finally, to prison, which was the federal satellite low at Jesup, Georgia. Figure that you will be going through at least one transfer center before arriving at your designated facility. Naturally, the farther away your prison is, the more transfer centers you will pass through. Eighteen months after being in Jesup, I was transferred to Miami FCI via Tallahassee.

You will get your first taste of what it is like to be at a federal prison once you arrive at your first transfer site. In many cases, you will be put in to a cell and will have to be locked down during certain parts of the day, but for the most part, you will be free to use whatever is available to you at the center. You will notice that your meals are much better and that the commissary list is more extensive. You will be allowed to go outside every day and will find that there is much more to do. There will be television to watch and books to read. If you have any money on your "books," you will be able to make phone calls usually within the first day, but not for a few hours until after your arrival. It will be at your transfer facility where you will finally be told where your final destination will be. Most men find that once they find out, they can begin asking around and will usually find other inmates at the transfer site that had done time at the place where they are going. You should do that too because it will give you an idea of what to expect. Remember, you are dealing with all different types of men or women, and they all have different opinions of where they have been. For instance, once I found out that I was going to Miami FCI, I began asking around about the prison. Some men loved it, and some did not. Most of what forms their opinions has to deal with the amount of time they spend at each facility. I had found out that Miami FCI was much better than Jesup FSL, but at Miami, we would be locked in our cells for standing counts and overnight, whereas at Jesup, you are in open dorms. I was told that the food was better at Miami, along with education, recreation, and commissary. I also found out the prices at the store were cheaper.

The one thing all the men who were at Miami told me is that at Miami, there is a lake. Miami FCI is the only federal prison that encircles a lake. The original Club Fed. As far as Florida standards go, it is actually a huge retention pond, but a body of water nonetheless. So ask around and keep an open mind. You now know where you are headed, and who knows how many more stops you will have to make along the way. The good thing is that your final destination will be within reach and you will be able to settle into a routine once and for all. Like the bus trips you had taken in the past, you will once again get processed out and issued a set of bus clothes. You may even get to fly on Con Air, which is an old 727. The leather seats are pretty beat-up, and there are no flight attendants to see to your every need, just a bunch of hard-nosed US marshals. You will remain cuffed and shackled, and if you are lucky, you may get some bottled water and a package of crackers. Whatever you do, do not let any part of your body or head lean out into the aisle, for a not-so-friendly US marshal will smack you in the head or knock your arm, leg, or shoulder out of the way. Ouch!

Getting back to the bus ride, one thing that you will **want to do** is ask the marshals transporting you to your next destination if they need a bus orderly. As the bus orderly, you will be responsible for passing out the bag meals and getting water for the inmates traveling with you on the bus. You will also be responsible for collecting all the trash left behind when everyone exits the bus. If you are doing your job during the ride, the amount of trash left behind will not be that much. Sounds like fun? That is not the reason why you volunteered. As the bus orderly, you get to travel without the encumbrance of handcuffs, chains, and shackles. Nothing sucks more than an eight-hour drive all chained up. You cannot stretch your head or even pick your nose. So remember these words, "Sir, I would like to volunteer to be the bus orderly." To ensure that your chances are good, always try to find a way to be toward the front of the group as you work your way through intake and the processing-out area. As trivial as this may seem, this is one perk that you will be glad you had. The bus will bring you to another transfer site, the airport, or to your prison. If it is to your prison, good luck and remember to use your eyes and your ears 95 percent of the time, and your mouth, the other 5 percent.

YOU HAVE FINALLY ARRIVED AT
YOUR DESTINATION—PRISON

The bus pulls in to the unloading area of your new home, for the next eighteen months at least, and it can be at any time of the day or night. Naturally, one would love to arrive during the day so that they can get situated and acclimated a little bit before going to sleep for the night. Depending on the time, you may have a meal waiting for you, and it will most likely be a bag lunch or dinner consisting of a sandwich, pretzels, cookies, and a drink. You may get lucky and be sent to your cell before a meal and get to eat with the inmates. That is the least of your worries. Just like everywhere else you have been for the past few weeks or months, you will have to fill out piles of paperwork, get fingerprinted—again for the hundredth time—and go through yet another full-body and cavity search. Hopefully, this will be the last one for many men.

After you are "checked" in, you get to speak with a doctor, psychologist, or PA to go over whatever ailments you have and to make sure your prescription drugs followed you from your last holdover. Once assigned a building (unit) and a cell, you will make your way to the laundry facility to pick up your bedroll, sheets, pillow (if any are available), and some clothing items, such as briefs, socks, shoes, T-shirts, and a poncho for foul weather.

You finally make it to your cell and meet your new cellys. Hopefully, you will be able to get along with each other. The BOP is supposed to put people together with those of their own persuasion, but it does not happen. Blacks are with whites, who are with Mexicans, who are with Columbians, who are with whites. This is the cause of some unrest among inmates, but usually, after a time and respect is shown on all ends by all parties involved, living with other races becomes acceptable.

Just like with anything new, it will take a lot of getting used to. Give it time, and you will be a pro at being able to do anything, be it legal or illegal. It is all a matter of survival.

The traveling and stay overs in transfer sites are no longer (unless you request a transfer in eighteen months or are moved). You are at your new home for the time being, and now is when the actual fight for your life begins.

YOU WILL BE JUDGED

Unless you are 6'5" and weigh 225 pounds, you will be judged by all the men at your facility. If you do happen to meet those physical requirements or are close to them, it will not matter if you are black, white, Hispanic, Asian, or whatever, for you will have a physical advantage over most of the men you are among, and in that case, you will have it a little easier than most. I have seen big men get the crap kicked out of them though, so do not think you will be immune to violence. Not many men fall into the above description, so I know it is safe to say that you need to be reading this book. The same goes for women.

In prison, if you are not black, you fall into the minority. If you are black, then consider yourself with an edge in the fight for survival.

The saying "Strength comes in numbers" is true in prison, and if you never get into an altercation with a black inmate, feel lucky. What you do not want to do is even think of it. Look around, you are in a sea of ebony—enough said. On the other hand, if you are a black inmate reading this, feel good in a sense that you will not be judged as severely as if you were not black.

Age and size play a huge part in how other prisoners look at you. Naturally, if you are younger, you are seen as somewhat of a threat due to the fact that you are stronger and most likely in better shape than most of the older inmates are. That gives you a slight advantage depending on the type of facility you are going to. In a low or a camp, you should be fine, but if going to a medium- or maximum-security prison, you will be singled out as a sex object, and you will have to deal with that problem when it arises. In most lows, satellite lows, and camps, you will not have that problem, seeing as most inmates are close to either going home, going to a camp, or heading to a halfway house, and they do not want to jeopardize that opportunity by doing anything that would raise their custody points and ruin any chances they have in going to a lower-security facility or going home. In all prisons, you have exceptions, and there is always that one knucklehead or two that will screw it up for everyone. While you may be in a low or lower, you still need to be aware of everything that goes on around you.

If you are an older inmate, you do not have to worry too much about being sexually abused but, instead, need to worry about being taken advantage of, especially if someone finds out that you have money in your inmate account. Actually, sex abuse is not very prevalent in the Fed, or at least not in minimum-security facilities or camps. Consensual sex is a different story. I have walked by the showers at 3:00 a.m. to go to the john and have seen two sets of feet in the shower stalls on quite a few occasions. I am not saying forcible sex does not happen, but it is not like what you see in the movies or on TV. Plus, what one sees on TV or in the movies is usually dealing with higher-security facilities.

If you are small in stature or overweight, you have a disadvantage the minute you walk onto the prison grounds. Small men and women along with obese inmates are seen as ones who cannot defend themselves as easily if you were in better shape, and that opens up the door for others to take advantage of you all the time. You must be able to stand up for yourself and not give in to threats so that others can get at your personal belongings, your commissary, or other items of worth to you. Once you give in to one person, you will be seen as a target. The threats and extortion will never go away until you decide to take some kind of action. Usually, it ends up with someone being physically injured or you being labeled as a snitch due to you going to the police or "dropping paper." When inmates find out that you are a snitch, and they will, your life has just become much more difficult, and everyone on the compound will avoid you and/or persecute you. Next to being a child molester, a snitch is the worst type of individual there is in prison.

If you are a tiny person or overweight, the best thing you can do is to mind your own business and try to stay below the radar as much as possible. With regard to being overweight, now is the time to do something about that. First, you will improve your overall health, and second, you will alter your physical image, and for most people, that will play a huge advantage when you are finally released from prison.

All federal prisons have a pretty extensive recreation department, which offers many avenues for one to be able to take off weight. You can use the weight-training facilities or stationary bikes; you can walk the track every day or even take classes aimed at losing weight. Some men even charge (usually about four stamps per session) to act as a personal trainer. You will have 100 percent control over your diet by either making your own meals each day or by utilizing food service on the compound. The choice is yours, and it should not be that difficult a choice at all.

Naturally, there are a few exceptions to the rule, and some men leave prison heavier than when they arrived. That is due to being excessively lazy. I have seen it happen. With so much time on your hands, it is very easy to get out and walk a few miles every day. If you can do that and stick to a decent diet, the weight will fall off quickly and you will begin to feel a little better about yourself, even if in a bad place. So yes, even though you are in a place you would rather not be, prison does have one or two advantages. I always laugh to myself when I think about what my best friend, Mike P., said to me in one of his letters, "Wouldn't it have been easier to join WeightWatchers?" So true. Seeing as I was in prison, I made the best of my time and gave it my best effort in trying to lose some weight. I lost thirty pounds by the time I walked out the prison gates in Spring of 2010. I still need to lose another seventy, and I could have lost it all when I was "down," but I let my guard down and made some unnecessary commissary purchases. I paid for it by not losing weight as quickly as I could have if I had been more disciplined. If I would have been able to lose that much weight, I would have changed my appearance drastically for the good, and other inmates would have seen me in a whole different light, and I know I would have been subject to less scorn and ridicule.

Remember: the color of your skin, your nationality, age, and weight will all have a bearing on how you will be treated by other inmates once you are in prison.

Now for the big one. Your charges will play a huge part in how others treat you. If you are in prison for murder, no problem. Robbed a bank? You're a hero. Drug dealer or drug user? Join the majority of inmates. Bilked your company of millions? Mail or wire fraud? You will be tolerated.

But if you are in prison for any type of sex offense, you will need to be very careful every day that you draw a breath. Sex offenders are like lepers. No one wants to associate with you (except other sex offenders), and everyone wants to harm you in one way or another. You will be the target of much verbal abuse and, in some instances, physical violence.

You could have just been fooling around on the Internet, or you could have molested young children—it does not matter. In prison, you will be labeled a cho-mo, prison speak for child molester. Once you have that moniker, your life behind the razor wire will become increasingly more difficult.

I am sure your counsel has already told you this, but I will reiterate it and will remind you throughout this book: ***do not tell anyone what your charges are***—period. If they are sex related, keep your mouth shut and tell no one. If they are related to any other type of crime, it is best that you say nothing because there are men in the system that will ask you about your case and charges and try to use it to their advantage. The prison system is full of snitches, and it does not stop at pretrial. If someone were to brag to another inmate where money is hidden from a robbery or tells another how he shot someone and got away with it, unfortunately, there are inmates that will go right to the authorities with this info in hopes of having their sentence reduced, even after conviction. The FBI will use anyone to help bolster their cases and even go as far as create stories to tell their snitches so that their charges stick. The best way is to have someone on the inside gather information that helps their cases.

Believe me when I tell you this: it is not worth it to let the entire prison population know why you are behind the razor wire, even if you didn't do it. It's funny how so many men I spoke with and knew in prison said they didn't do it—yeah, right!

If you are a sex offender, what I am about to tell you next is probably the most important thing you can do when going to prison. Not only are you reading it here in my book, but somewhere along the way, your counsel will most likely mention this as well as the first few people that interview you when you arrive at your destination prison. These people are usually the facility psychologist, a physician's assistant (PA), and your unit manager. They will tell you this: If you are in prison for a sex offense, it would be best if you come up with some other type of charge that you can tell others if you are asked why you are there or if you feel compelled to let others know. The sucky part is that you will be in a catch-22 situation because if you refuse to tell others what you are in for, most automatically peg you as a sex offender because all others tell what they are serving time for without even batting an eyelash—except snitches and sex offenders. In many instances, you will come across inmates who will want you to show some sort of paperwork showing what your charges are to make sure you are not a cho-mo. It is sad that it has come to this, but you will find this archaic way of rationalization at every prison at every level. There is no reasoning with these Neanderthals, and you will find out that a few of these vigilantes were drug dealers that had no problem selling drugs to nine and ten-year-olds. Go figure! If you can, see if your counsel would be willing to put together some type of documentation that could be sent to you as soon as you arrive at your prison that shows your "new" charges. If your counsel will not put together some type of legal documents for you, you can make them yourself. You can use the law library at your prison and take an existing document and change some of the information on it. When anyone asks for any type of proof as to why you are in prison, just show them your "documentation." Only one person needs to know your made-up charges, and word will spread quickly that you are not a cho-mo. The best way to put an end to any speculation as to what your charges are is to show them. Just telling someone is not going to get it done. It is unfortunate that you would have to lie like that, but it is all part of your survival plan. This only pertains to those convicted of sex offenses. Almost any other crime will not bring attention to you unless you go looking for it and bring trouble upon yourself.

As you are aware of, prisons are very transient. Every week, men and women are leaving as well as entering. Within a few months' time, the population will change so much that you constantly have to be aware of whom you are dealing with. You will always be asked that dreaded question, "What are you here for?" throughout your tenure in prison. Most of you don't have to worry, but for sex offenders and snitches, be sure you are in prison for any charge other than your real ones and do what is necessary to back that up, comprende?

OK, you went ahead and got yourself some pretty convincing documentation and they seem to be working. I must tell you this: there are other ways for others to find out your charges without you telling them or showing them. It can be as easy as looking at the computer screen in your counselor's office if he or she has left your information up on their screen. I have seen others' information many times, and after a while, one knows exactly where to look on the screen for charges. People can have others look up individuals on the Internet through certain law-enforcement websites or on BOP.gov. All that is needed is one's name or eight-digit inmate ID number. The inmate ID number is so easy to obtain because it is on all your clothing and on the morning callout sheet every day. You also must list it on any sign-up sheet that you put your name on. It is sad to say, but in my facility and in others throughout the country, I am sure there are prison officers and administrators that will tell inmates information that they shouldn't, and many times, it is about another person's charges.

If you feel that your cover has been blown, like they say on TV, then the next best thing for you to do is not give the inmate population any ammunition to use against you. From the day you arrive at your institution, remain proactive and productive and make as few friends as possible while trying to remain as visible as you can. Make your visibility a good visibility.

In addition to your charges, age, appearance, race, and sometimes, religion all play a huge part in how you are perceived and judged once you arrive at your prison. If you are in good physical shape, young, and black, you automatically have an advantage over most other men, like I had mentioned earlier. If you are white or any other race than black, you need to be in good shape, physically fit, and in prison for any charges other than being a government informant or a sex offender. I was an overweight white forty-nine-year-old and prematurely gray, so I decided to shave my head. While I was not the most menacing inmate in prison, I never encountered any violence and have never been taken advantage of due to my age, color, or size. That one alteration to my appearance helped a little; I am sure.

Remember, the first thing another inmate will do is judge you by your outward appearance and then attempt to intimidate you and see how easy or difficult a mark you will be. If you are not a specimen of perfect health and stature, you are already at a disadvantage and will need to act in order to remain safe and sane. If you have half a brain, and I am sure you do, it will not be that difficult to survive prison, even if you are a cho-mo or snitch. If you are stubborn and feel you need to be in control, I feel sorry for you.

DAMNED IF YOU DO, DAMNED IF YOU DON'T
(For sex offenders and snitches)

Once it is proven what you are in for, life will become a little easier for you. If not a sex offender or snitch, you can feel some relief that you don't have to fight other battles besides ones dealing with size and color.

You've proven your charges, be they real or made up, and people accept you. It is now up to you how much attention you want to draw upon yourself, be it good or bad. Naturally, you want to draw as little attention if possible, but if you do, make sure it is positive.

In some instances, you will have to let some people know what you are in for. Many times, when lying in your bunk, a celly may ask you, and you should tell him, for you will be living with this person for some time. It will be totally up to you if you continue your charade or come clean and hope that your celly(s) will accept you afterward.

I have seen some sex offenders come right out and tell the truth, and in some cases, they were not messed with for they were not drawing attention to themselves. You walk a very thin line and will have to decide how you want to go about handling what your charges are. You can do as the administration has instructed you to do and fabricate some charges other than your real ones, or you could tell the truth right from the start and hope for the best. I'd fabricate charges if I were you.

All you have to do is rub someone the wrong way or get someone upset with you, and the next thing you know, they are making inquiries about you to someone they know on the outside. If you have something to hide, you will be found out.

I have seen it work both ways with regard to coming clean. One guy who remained to himself and did not bother anyone was left alone, but another guy who had a big mouth and went to the police, even if someone looked at him the wrong way, was beaten up and had things done to him and his property. The choice is yours, and it is a hard choice to make, but nobody said prison was going to be a picnic, and by no means is prison fair. Everyone is there for doing **something** wrong, yet the inmates have their own sets of rules and ethics that you cannot fight. The best thing to do is to use your brain to find ways to outsmart them in order to find ways to survive.

So, sex offenders or snitches, you have a hard decision to make, but I am sure you will do what is right and what will keep you out of trouble.

When I got to prison, I was one of the worst stereotypes imaginable. I was nearly fifty years old, white, overweight, and out of shape. I know that God had watched over me every step of the way, and I also know that I did not encounter any abuse because of the way I carried myself over the thirty-six months in prison and eighteen months of federal custody. Here are two words that you must remember in order to stay out of trouble: proactive and productive.

PATIENCE
WHAT?
ANOTHER LINE?

One virtue that you will learn when you come to prison is patience. If you are an impatient person, you had better be able to adapt, or else, you will find yourself getting into trouble over the littlest things and your already stressed-out stress level will go even higher. Who wants to have a heart attack because they are last for meals every day? It's not worth punching someone out for cutting in front of you to take a crap.

Everything you do in prison usually has some sort of wait or line. There is no getting around it. From the moment you are arrested and taken into custody, your life of waiting on lines has begun. You will wait on a line for **EVERYTHING.** Get used to it.

Remember just one thing—you are in prison and you are not going anywhere right away anyhow.

Most all prisons are overcrowded, even in the Fed, which means you will most likely be in a facility that has been designated for hundreds if not thousands less than what it could comfortably (I don't say legally for there is no legal in the Fed for they make up their own rules) hold. The BOP does not give a damn about this overcrowding because every year, it just gets worse and worse even though Congress says that they are trying to figure out ways to rid the system of overcrowding. Yeah, right! The BOP is a huge moneymaker for the US government. I will not go into that because I can take another twenty pages on that subject alone. I am only trying to help you survive your duration behind the concertina wire.

At my first facility, Jesup FSL, it was originally designated as a camp for about 180 inmates. It is now a federal satellite low that houses over 600. While the population has more than tripled, the facilities have remained the same. Each floor that used to house 30 inmates now houses almost 80. The same 4 toilet stalls and 4 showers are now being used by three times the amount of men they were designed for. The same goes for the 3 urinals and 7 sinks. Eighty men have to share 1 microwave oven, 1 water fountain, 1 washer, and 1 dryer. This is not just at Jesup, but nationwide in the Fed and much worse in higher-security prisons.

So wherever you are going, be prepared to wait on line to do everything, from taking a leak to taking a shower; from heating up dinner to brushing your teeth; from sending an e-mail to a loved one to waiting for medical attention, even in emergency situations.

What I just mentioned represent the short wait times.

Meal? Forget about it. Figure anywhere from five minutes to fifteen minutes every time you go to the dining hall to eat. That is when your unit is called out for meals. Units are supposedly sent to meals according to how well they do in weekly inspections. The same units always go first, and the others follow in line. If your unit is last, you go to meals about forty minutes after chow is called. You get what is left, if there is anything left.

On days when they serve chicken, everyone eats, so figure you will wait about twenty to twenty-five minutes to just get in the door.

Have to see the doctor? Sick? Can't breathe? Have some sort of rash? Diarrhea? Chest pains? Cough? Fill out a sick-call notice and go wait on line. You will be given an appointment, which may not even be for that day, and then you come back and wait in line again. Need pills, insulin, or medication? Every morning and every evening, there is what is called pill line. There's that word again—line. Get in line to get your meds, and figure an upward of an hour on some days.

You will find that over time, these lines do not seem to bother you anymore. You find yourself bringing a book to read or you just chalk it up to experience. Patience. You have become a more patient individual. See how easy it is? Too bad that it took having to go to prison to find out that it is a good thing to be able to have patience.

Occasionally, you will see a few inmates get into a shoving match or playing a "boo game" on one another for cutting in line or not being patient, but you will see that in most cases, these are inmates that had just arrived and do not know any better. In time, they will fall in line. There's that word again.

DOING TIME REQUIRES THAT YOU USE YOUR EYES AND EARS 95 PERCENT OF THE TIME AND YOUR MOUTH THE OTHER 5 PERCENT

For many men and women, the hardest thing about doing time is keeping their mouths shut. You will see many things that do not agree with your way of thinking. You will look at how you were brought up and say to yourself that what is happening is so far from what you have learned about right and wrong for wrong is the norm in prison. Your natural reaction will be to tell someone. Don't!

You will see inmates stealing from food service on a daily basis. You will see men stealing from other inmates. In the rec yard and even in your unit, you will find men sneaking a smoke, be it cigarettes or pot. You will see men drinking and getting drunk, fighting, damaging property—the list goes on. Guess what? It is none of your business. The biggest mistake an inmate can make is that they make the above-mentioned issues their business. If you are not directly involved, stay out of it. If you see something or hear something, leave it at that. Use your eyes and ears only.

Once you begin to try to change things (things that have been this way long before you arrived and will be that way long after you leave), you will be labeled a snitch, and all of a sudden, bad things will begin to happen to you. Guess what? No one will have seen or heard anything with regard to the bad things that come your way.

Everyone who goes to prison for the first time has the I-am-going-to-tell attitude. It is difficult to let these events just take their course, but it is something that you will have to chalk up to experience. Prisons are filled with bad people, and they have their own rules and codes of ethics (talk about oxymoron). Believe me, they do. You will not agree with many of them, but they are there, and they are enforced.

If you are a black man or woman, be glad, for in prison, you are the majority. In a way, you run what goes on from day to day. White, Hispanic, Asian, European, or whatever, if you are not black, you have no say in what goes on unless you decide to go to the police and try to change things. Sure, you will see change for a short time, but things will just revert to how they were in the past, and now, you will be a target. You do not want that.

You will hear all the time when you are in prison the saying "The animals run the zoo." It is sad, but it is true. We are all behind the razor wire and bars, but in a way, the police are just there to baby-sit. Give it time, and you will see that it is the inmates that run everything; you'll see. Because the majority of inmates are black, guess what? It all comes down to the blacks running the operation. If you are not black, then just shut up and do your time.

Like I said, it will be hard at first to not want to speak up or want to change things. If you can roll with the flow, you will see that your time will go quickly and you will not be bothered or harassed. Even if you are a government informant or a cho-mo, as long as you don't make any waves and keep your "friends" to a minimum, you should not have any problems making it through your sentence in one piece. Again, it is totally up to you how you handle yourself in prison. The loudmouths and the ones that constantly disregard authority will be put in their place by the police or fellow inmates; you can be sure of that. Whatever you do, don't give anyone the ammunition they need to come after you. You give them the "bullets," and they will use them; you give them nothing, and they will leave you alone.

You always want to be listening and watching out all the time. While it is not in your best interest to go running to the police every time you hear or see something that is not how it should be, it is definitely a smart thing to remember who the people are that are doing the bad things. You will soon learn to avoid these people and their associates, and you will find your time will go smoother and without incident.

DO NOT purposely try to listen in on another's conversation or spy on others because this is known as ear hustling and eye hustling, and inmates that are found to do that usually end up having some part of their anatomy rearranged. The best way to go through prison when you feel or know something is not right is to abide by the old adages: "Speak only when spoken to" and "Be seen and not heard."

DO YOU REALLY MAKE FRIENDS IN PRISON?

You will hear many people say that while in prison, they do not make any friends. Heed this advice, and life will be easier on the outside once you are released. Think about it—while you may get close to your cell mate(s) and others, do you really want to consider them as friends? Once you are behind the razor wire, you will see that it is not a wise thing to make friends. Associates, yes, but friends, no. I am sure there are always exceptions. Rare, I am sure.

Think about it—you are among criminals, and when you get out, do you really want to remain in touch with these individuals? While you are on supervised release (probation), you will not be allowed to associate with these people anyway. It is best to distance yourself immediately once you arrive at your prison.

In many cases, men want to get close to you for their own selfish motives, and a lot of times, it is because they want something from you. It may be commissary, an address of one of your good-looking girlfriends or even your ex-wife, the newspaper you get daily, or even for drugs that are prescribed to you.

Men who have means of support on the outside must be very careful not to let others know you have a flow of funds into your inmate account; for once men know you have "money," your friends will come out of the woodwork.

Choose the men you want to hang with very carefully because you will find that some of them are not whom you think they are. I don't want to tell you to be a loner, but it may not be bad advice. It will be very difficult to not associate with anyone, but the fewer people you get close to, the better off you will be. If you can keep your circle of "friends" to five or six, you will be OK.

IT IS NOT THE "REAL WORLD" BEHIND THE RAZOR WIRE

Once you spend a little time in the Fed, you will see that life is nothing like what it was when you were on the outside. On the outside, there was order and a way to get things done. In prison, it is more like controlled chaos, and every time you think you have it figured out as to how things are getting done, something changes.

Patience goes a long way in all aspects of prison life. Every day, you have to deal with corrections officers and administrators, and each of these people does things their own way. One would think that these people have a defined set of rules they have to adhere to (they do), but many of them make up their own rules, and the BOP looks the other way.

Some of these superiors are more lax than others while others are much stricter. Every day is different, and in time, you will know who the good staff is and who is not so good.

Some examples, on some days, there will be open moves all day, while on others, the compound will be subject to ten-minute moves on every hour at the half hour. One dining room CO will allow inmates to get back in line for seconds, while another will make sure you only get what the menu calls for and nothing more. Some will open up the libraries or classrooms in advance of a clerk being there while others will not.

The best thing to do is ignore the COs that go by the rules and not say anything to them or anyone else about how other

COs do things for you. If you do, eventually, word will get back to administration, and you will jeopardize what the more lax COs do for you. It is better to go back for seconds two times a week than no times at all, understand?

On the outside, you have cash, checks, and credit cards. In prison, you have stamps. That is the latest form of currency. In the past it used to be macs, or mackerel, for the canned fish costs $1 at most commissaries, and that made for easy transactions. The BOP has done away with the can, and the cost is now over $1.

You want to get something from the "store man"—get your cell cleaned, laundry done, or even buy cigarettes? You pay with stamps. Either that or you purchase items at commissary in return for services rendered.

It is not permitted to purchase items or services from other inmates or for other inmates, but you will see that this is an ongoing practice that has been going on for a long time. If you happened to see the movie *The Shawshank Redemption*, try to remember the Morgan Freeman character, Red. Every prison has a Red, someone who can get just about anything for anyone.

Some days, you will wake up and say to yourself, "What am I doing here?" Everything will seem so surreal to you. You are sleeping in a room with virtually one or two (and sometimes more) complete strangers. You are living among men that have committed murder, robbed banks, raped children, sold and used drugs, bilked their companies of millions, and so much more. Now you are one of the gang, and you just shake your head sometimes. You must adapt to their rules, or you will get singled out and ostracized. You will have to play their game the way they mean for it to be played, not the way the BOP tells you. You step out of line, and you will wish you were in the "hole" or at another facility.

You may not feel like there is much stress on you for you get three meals a day and have a bed to sleep in. Take one look around you and take a look in the mirror. You and the men with you get grayer much faster in prison. For many men, it was not long ago when they arrived, but it looks like they were there forever. Prison takes its toll on everyone, and it will be up to you how much you want it to take out of you. It is a completely different world on the inside. Try to adapt as quick as you can and realize this IS real. Do that, and you should be OK.

HOW CAN YOU BE PROACTIVE AND PRODUCTIVE IN PRISON? GET A JOB!

After about two weeks at your new prison, you will be required to find a job. Yes, you read that correctly; you will need to find work, and yes, you will get paid. Not much, but you will make some money, nonetheless.

At every federal prison, there are not enough jobs for everyone, so you will have to get friendly with one of the corrections officers and hope that he or she can fit you to their work detail. Or you can just kick back and let your unit team assign you to a work detail, and I will tell you for a fact that the job they give you will be in food service.

If you luck out and are put on a work detail that you specifically asked to be on, you are among the minority. Most men work their way to their current positions through working in the kitchen first.

Eighty-five percent of the jobs in prison are so easy that after a while, the inmates do not even report in and the ones that do report end up doing all the work. After a while, this gets old and there is usually some sort of confrontation between the workers and the slackers. If you think you are getting away with not showing up for work, you are wrong. The COs and the staff know your every move when it comes to work detail.

If you have no way of receiving funds from the outside and feel uncomfortable running your own hustle, then it may be worth your while to get a job that pays more than what the other 85 percent of all the other inmates are making. You can ask around and find that just about everyone you know is making maintenance pay, and that comes out to $5.25 per month. Yep, you read that correctly, $5.25 a month. You will notice that these inmates making $5.25 a month are the ones that are working "created" jobs by officers that they got close to and that the required time to be on the job is about fifteen minutes per day. Not much of a job, huh? Working only fifteen minutes a day makes for a slow tenure in prison. It would be in your best interest to find a job that pays you for at least five hours' work a day.

If you have a certain talent or learned trades, such as A/C repair, plumbing, carpentry, electrical, etc., then you can become a part of CMS, which is the prison maintenance group made up strictly of inmates. These laborers make anywhere from $12 to $50 a month, depending on how often their services are needed.

Food Service

Do you like to cook or bake? Then by all means try to get a job in the kitchen. In some prisons, there are three shifts, and in others, there are two. Either way, you can almost guarantee working about forty hours, and that makes your time pass quickly. The prisons that have three shifts staff their kitchens as follows: Morning shift works five days a week from 4:30 a.m. to 11:30 a.m. Cooks, cook's assistants, and bakers work the entire shift, while line servers, table and floor cleaners, and dishwashers work about four hours with a two—to three-hour break between breakfast and lunch. Cooks, cook's assistants, and bakers make about $70.00 per month while line servers and those with abbreviated hours make $5.25 to about $12.00 per month. If you have no problems waking up early, the preferred shift to work in food service is the morning shift. The afternoon shift works from 11:30

a.m. to 6:30 p.m., with the main workers staying the entire shift while the support workers leave after lunch cleanup and come back to serve dinner. The relief crew works two morning shifts and two evening shifts, and this is the second preferred shift in food service.

I worked the morning shift for over three years and can honestly tell you, if you want to make a positive impression on many inmates, then try to get one of the main cooking positions or the baker's job. It is these inmates that put together ten meals a week (morning shift), and it is these meals that are talked about the most, day after day. Do a good job, and you will become everyone's best friend. If you are perceived as doing a bad job, you can always blame the poor quality of your baked goods on the food service administrator for giving you an inferior product to work with, so you don't look bad either way. Breakfast and lunch are the two most-eaten meals on the compound, and for the most part, you have enough material to make decent meals. I lucked into my position as baker and was quickly made the lead baker. Anyone with any common sense and who knows how to read and follow directions can be the compound baker. If you decide to go that route and be a baker, here is the secret to keeping the inmate population happy at lunchtime: *frosting.*

In many institutions, the kitchen makes cakes in a hurry and either puts powdered sugar or a meager drizzle icing on their cakes. I found out that if you put frosting on your cakes, the inmates love it. Most men and women have not had cakes with frosting in a long time, and if your dining room supervisor allows it (which he/she should), then go for it every day that you make cakes. Vary your desserts, and the inmates will soon like the fact that the baker is on their side. What it really comes down to is taking a little pride in what you are doing and not stealing or having ulterior motives for being in the kitchen.

Yes, you are in prison, and nobody seems to care about anything or anyone, but do your job and do it well, and people will notice, and this recognition will be positive. It is always nice to know that most of the compound will have your back if a problem were to ever arise between you and another inmate. For me, it was being a good baker. For others, it may be being a good electrician or plumber and making sure things are fixed and work right. If you can get a highly visible job that affects a lot of inmates, then get it, because nine times out of ten, if you do your job correctly, you will get nothing but positive recognition, and that goes a long way in prison.

Another great thing about having a job that takes up about eight hours a day is that your time goes much faster, and not only do inmates see you as a good worker, but so does the administration. The more visible you are to those that matter, the better off you will be, as long as that visibility does not center on getting into trouble.

I am not saying you do not get a fifteen-minute compound job, for it may be the only thing available or you may like having a job where nobody cares what you do. Just make sure that you do your fifteen minutes every day because there are inmates that do "care" about what you do, and it is these nosy inmates that will make your life miserable. It is these inmates that have to know what everyone else is doing, and sooner than later, you will hear, "Hey, so-and-so is a compound orderly, and he hasn't lifted a finger to do any work in three months." Believe me, everyone knows what everyone else is doing, but it is a few that make it known to the police. Once you get that type of lazy reputation, that is when the rumors begin, and you will soon hope that those eyes your mother has/had behind her head begin to show up on the back of yours.

Recreation Jobs

Almost every federal prison has an extensive recreation facility, and just about every institution has softball, basketball, football, and soccer. If you have any experience officiating in any of those sports, then by all means, see your compound recreation officer. At first, I figured you had to be crazy to be a softball umpire or basketball official. Hell, you are among criminals playing sports that need officiating, and what would happen to an official if he makes a wrong call? Actually, prison sports are run with very strict rules, and the inmates are serious about their sports, so you do not have to take it literally when someone in the stands yells, "Kill the umpire!"

No matter how bad a game you may have called, you will walk off the field in one piece. The trick is to not call a bad game. If you have enough experience, then there should be no reason to call bad games. Yes, everyone misses a call here and there, but as long as the inmates and guards see you hustling and in the right position to make the call, you will never have a problem—OK, well, almost never. After umpiring my first two prison games, all six softball teams were asking the league commissioner if the "fat guy" could call their games. I was nonbiased, and the men liked that. They saw that I showed no favoritism and that I knew the rules of the game. Oh yes, you will find officials in all the leagues that will make calls for their homeys. Stay away from doing that, and you will be fine.

One bonus is that the pay is pretty decent. Most places pay per game, and the pay is about $2.00 for umpiring and refereeing; $1.50 for keeping the scorebook; and $0.50 to $1.00 to keep the scoreboard. It adds up, and over a season, you can make an additional $25.00 to $50.00 a month. One thing that I did was to do the league statistics each week for both basketball and softball. I would post league and individual stats each week and was paid additionally for that. A big bonus for doing weekly stats is that all the players become your "friend" because they all want to know how they are doing and love comparing themselves to their homeys. It also keeps you busy for many months out of the year. (Note: At Miami FCI, they pay officials with sodas and not nearly what they promise for the recreation officer and his inmate supervisor have to take their "cut.")

Education

Know how to play a musical instrument? Taught or tutored on the outside? Have a college degree? Know about real estate? Acting?

Language arts? If you have any type of talent or skill that you want to pass on to others and are proficient at that skill, then you can teach in prison. Almost all classes are taught by inmates where some are volunteer positions while others are paid through the Education Department. Either way, you will get a great deal of personal satisfaction out of teaching twenty inmates what you know in a specific field. You set up the curriculum, put together a syllabus, and off you go. Most classes run for about ten weeks. Go for it!

Don't want to teach? You can work as a clerk in either of the two libraries on most prison compounds. Most have both a leisure library and a law library. Many of the library jobs do not pay that much, but you get to work for about six to eight hours a day, and that makes your time go by quickly.

Commissary and Laundry

These two jobs pay pretty well compared to most other jobs on the compound, but not many inmates are needed to fill the positions for both jobs, and in many cases, in order to work in either commissary or in laundry, you need to be in tight with a guard or supervisor. Laundries only have about ten inmates working there and even less for commissary in most prisons. Usually, from four to ten inmates work at the store. The one nice thing about working in either job is that there are nice perks.

CMS

Every prison has what is called CMS, which is where you will find your carpenters, plumbers, and electricians. All these positions are held by inmates, and the pay is often quite good by prison standards. Be prepared to be on call if you apply and are accepted in to a CMS job.

UNICOR (Prison Industries)

This is where the big money is made. If you want to take home a check from $150 to $400 a month, then you want to work in UNICOR. That is if you don't mind working for the US government, the same group of guys that put you in prison to begin with. UNICOR is the manufacturing arm of the government that is made up strictly of inmates. Most prisons manufacture furniture, textiles, and electronics while some do graphic work and design for the armed forces and other government agencies. Pay at UNICOR ranges anywhere from $0.23 an hour up to $1.35 an hour. Some inmates can make over $500 per month when there is overtime involved. UNICOR takes or, should I say, chooses from three inmate groups: (1) those with fines and restitution, (2) those with prior UNICOR experiences, and (3) those who just want to work in UNICOR.

The bad thing about everyone wanting to work for UNICOR is that less than 20 percent of all federal inmates work in UNICOR, meaning if you are at a facility that houses about one thousand inmates, less than two hundred will be working for UNICOR. Figure out your own odds. There is a waiting list for each category, and it usually takes over a year or a year and one-half to get into UNICOR.

Watch the lists on a weekly or monthly basis, because UNICOR **_will_** hire whomever they want, list or no list. Like with other jobs on the compound, it is all about whom you know. Go to your UNICOR facility and walk around and meet the guards running it. Like on the outside, make yourself visible and even train on a piece of equipment with someone you know that is willing to show you. If the staff sees you are interested, when it becomes time for UNICOR to hire someone, magically, men's names move up the list. With the right connections and exposure, that name could be yours.

GAMBLING AND TELEVISIONS: THE TWO BIGGEST PROBLEMS YOU WILL ENCOUNTER WHILE IN PRISON

Gambling is a given, but the TVs? you ask. You will find that wherever you are, there are more arguments and fights over the TV than anything else on a prison compound. It all has to do with a limited number of television sets and an overpopulation of inmates. At one time, inmates were allowed to have their own television sets, and after that, before prisons became sardine cans, there were fewer men, and the problems were not as much. Now you have over one thousand inmates at each facility and less than twenty television sets, and that equals problems.

Each prison has individual TV rooms for Hispanic inmates, but the rest are up for grabs. Every prison has certain rooms and certain TV sets designated for different types of shows. While it is all well and good to have a sports TV room, a news TV room, and a movie room, if you are not black, then you better take up reading or look to do something a little more worthwhile, like walking the track or finding something else to take up your time other than TV.

If there are no sports on, figure on watching BET or soap operas. No movie or news? The same thing. Even if the news is on, or there is a movie you want to see, more than likely, you will not be able to watch it unless it deals with black issues.

If there is something on that you feel like watching, in most instances, you will have to stand in the back or put your chair off to the side somewhere because all the TV rooms have assigned seating, and most of these assigned seats are held by black inmates. As soon as the TV room becomes available, the inmates place their chairs in the room, even if they do not plan on watching anything for hours. Sometimes, you can get away with sitting in another man's chair, but in many instances, don't even bother unless you are looking for trouble.

Every unit has a television committee, but you can forget getting anywhere with them for they are always made up of black inmates or the majority are. Always keep this in the back of your mind when you are in prison: you are in a black man's world.

Do not make a scene about watching some TV show. You may win a battle here and there, but you will always lose the war. If you are a black inmate, your chance of watching a show of your choice goes up considerably. The best thing to do while spending time in prison is to try to avoid the television sets unless you can get to them around 5:30 a.m. when nobody is awake.

Gambling in prison is widespread. My best advice to you is to stay away from betting on sports or getting involved in a poker game. Usually, if you bet on a game of some sort, you will have to come up with the stamps before you bet and then trust whomever you bet with to pay you off if you win. On more than one occasion, I have seen prison bookies not pay off winners. You are in prison; you really think everyone is going to be honest when it comes to having to pay up? Most do make good, but you do have a few who don't, and that makes it bad for everyone.

Poker is the game of choice at every prison. Most games will run a week or two before the house collects from all the losers. Most of the time, you will lose. If you win, you have to rely on some loser to cover your winnings, even though it is the house's responsibility to make sure you get paid. Some of these games get so heated up that you will see many fights over a poker game.

If the police decide to shut your game down, you may be looking at time in the hole and lose good time, if they want to take it that far. Again, my advice is to stay away from the poker games, betting, and television. It may be difficult, but it will also keep you out of harm's way.

SMOKING, DRUGS, AND ALCOHOL

I am not going to lie and say that there is no smoking, drug use, or drinking going on in prison.

While the BOP has stopped smoking at all facilities, you can walk into any unit at most any time of the day and find an inmate puffing away on a cigarette in the bathroom or as far away from the unit officers or counselors' offices as they possibly can get. If not in the unit, then far out on the rec yard, behind a building, or even in one—you can always find someone "lit up."

The same goes for inmates that want to do a line of coke or light up a joint. Pot will be smoked outside the unit, usually on the rec yard, just like those smoking cigarettes. Inmates who snort cocaine are more daring and will do it in the unit on many occasions.

Drinking is done everywhere. Inmates will put their "homemade" alcohol in their water bottles and drink it on the compound and out on the rec yard. Just like being home in the hood.

One may ask, how does one get tobacco and drugs on the compound? Easy, contraband is brought in the prison by prison guards, staff, and office personnel. Not every prison official is a goody-goody. Like you see in the movies, someone is always on the take.

With regard to smoking, many guards and prison personnel smoke and do not abide by the prisons own rules and smoke wherever they want to. In many instances, it is on the compound where inmates are present. Once these individuals finish their smoke, they throw the butt on the ground. These butts are collected and opened, and eventually, the industrious inmate has enough tobacco to make a cigarette.

Some guards and staff leave cigarettes for inmates that are their snitches and pets. Others bring the contraband in and leave it for inmates in the inmates' cells or in areas designated by the agreement between the inmate and the one bringing in the contraband.

So while these vices are banned at every level in the Fed, it is freely being abused by many inmates, and these habits are being fueled by prison personnel that are looking for additional income or actually were once acquainted with the inmate on the outside.

Personally, I recommend that you quit smoking or use the downtime to try. Definitely stay away from the drugs and hooch. The choice is yours, but in the end, many of these offenders get caught, even the "good guys."

PRISON ETIQUETTE

If prison etiquette is not the biggest oxymoron, then I do not know what is. Anyway, you will need to conduct yourself in a way that you do not offend other inmates and especially your own cell mates. Remember, once you are in a federal prison, you are no longer dealing with transient cell mates like you may have experienced in county holdovers, etc. Depending on how well you get along with your new cellys and how long each of you have left on your sentences, you may be spending a long time with these individuals, and it is best that you know how to conduct yourself among strangers and, sometimes, "animals," for that is what they actually are.

In some instances, you will be sharing living quarters with someone who has been down for a long time, and they have certain ways in which things are done. In others circumstances, you and your celly(s) may be new to the system, and you will develop your own ways of doing things within your cell. If that is the case, you may want to inquire of some men who have been down for a while as to the right way to conduct yourself while sharing a cell, for all new cellys may continue to do things the way they did on the outside because on a lot of occasions, you always had someone to clean up after you. Well, my friend, it is time to finally grow up, and you will, quickly. You may not agree with some of the things that you see being done, but the sooner you learn to adapt, the better off you will be.

At the beginning of your tenure in the Fed, more than likely, you will be in a three-man cell. Once you can master living in a three-man with two complete strangers, the rest will or should come easy. As a matter of fact, once you do make it into a two-man cell, you will feel a huge load being lifted off your shoulders. You will find that you sleep better at night and there is going to be less stress in your life. In most cases, the objective is to get into a two-man as soon as you can. The easiest way to get in to a two-man, besides having a physical disability, is to just be good. It's that simple.

Unless you have a lower-bunk pass (medical pass excluding you from top racks), it is best that once you enter your cell for the first time, do not even ask your cellys "Where do you want me?" Just throw your bedding on the top bunk (unless that bunk is made up) and begin your tenure from the top. In many cases, the bunk that you will be using will only have a bare mattress, and that usually is a good indication of where you are going to be. If you are really not sure as to which bunk will be yours, go ahead and ask a celly.

All of a Sudden, Everyone Has Cooties

Introduce yourself and do not extend your hand unless one is extended to you for many men in prison refrain from touching other men or, more specifically, skin that may carry sickness and disease. You will notice a lot of men doing strange things with regard to having their skin come in contact with things. The most noticeable is that you will see men open doors by using their shirt or a towel. You will see men on the phone with a sock over the receiver. Can you say stupid? I guess they do not realize that germs can manifest themselves in dirty linens also. Duh. You do not have to go to those extremes and will find that you can open doors and talk on the phones as you did on the outside. Some men take things a bit too far, and the unfortunate thing is that they feel everyone else should too. Eventually, you will be able to tell the lunatics from the health conscious, and then the decisions are strictly up to you. While it is a good thing to disinfect toilet seats, phones, and door handles, it is really not necessary, and you may not always have disinfectant at your disposal.

Cramped Quarters

More than likely, you will be starting out in a top bunk and will need to get used to the cold air blowing on you at night, for many inmates believe that keeping the room cold keeps germs to a minimum—until the two or three of you come down with a cold or even worse.

Getting back to the layout of your cell, when in a three-man cell, you will see that there is only room for two men to sit comfortably at one time. There are three chairs yet only enough room for two. The man in the top bunk always has first choice where to sit and when, for it is easier for the man in the lower bunk to sit on his bed or lie in it to read or talk. The middle bunk has second choice, and if all three of you are in the cell at one time, the lower-bunk cell mate does not get to use a chair. There are exceptions, like when you are the only one in the cell and your two cellys come in afterward or if you need to use the desk.

Seeing that you are in a nine-by-twelve space and there is not much room to maneuver, even when you are alone, try doing it with three men in there at one time. My advice to anyone is to find things to do outside the cell and only use your cell to brush your teeth, take a crap, get dressed, and go to sleep. The worst thing one can do is make enemies with a cell mate, and then one of two things will happen: you'll end up getting into a fight or one of you (usually the newest celly) will have to find somewhere else to live. Musical cells is not a game you want to play for it gives the other inmates the impression that you are hard to get along with.

Nature Calls

There is nothing wrong with taking a pee while one or two of your cellys are in the cell with you. Just be sure to let them know, and when you are done, be sure to wipe down the toilet, and if you have some type of disinfectant, spray and wipe the toilet after each use. Afterward, be sure to wash your hands. Inmates pick up on every little thing others do or do not do. If they see that you do not wash after taking a pee or shower every day, they will not only let you know, but they will tell everyone else too, and then you will be labeled as a slob. Do not let that happen. Become a neat freak. Heck, you were supposed to be taught these things as you were growing up anyway.

What if you have to take a crap and one or two of your cellys are in the cell? You have to tell them you need to take a crap, and they will leave. If you're alone, then there is no issue. You will need to let others know that you are in your cell taking a crap so that no one comes and visits while you are on the can. It is called putting a flag up. Most inmates drape a towel over their door to cover the window while some use a strip of toilet tissue that they stick directly to the window. Most windows are thin and about the width of a sheet of toilet tissue. If you use toothpaste to "glue" the toilet tissue to the window, be sure to wipe it clean when you are done. You do not necessarily have to cover your window for men should not be looking in cells, but you need to put something out so that your cellys know the cell is being used by you. You can also, just wrap a piece of toilet tissue around the door handle or stick a piece out the door near the handle. Hanging a piece of toilet tissue on your door handle is the universal sign that the toilet is being used.

At home, you probably did not flush every time your crap hit the water, but in prison, be sure to put some water on it often. At home, you called it a courtesy flush, and in prison, you are putting water on it. Do not worry about wasting water, but instead, worry about the other two guys you are living with. Plus, the government is paying for the water, not you. Well, actually, it is the taxpayers who are paying.

If you know that your cellys are in the building, do not break out a book or newspaper to read while doing your business. Make it as quick as possible, and if you know they are at work or on the rec yard or whatever, then and only then can you take your time, but always remember to put water on it no matter what. When you are through, clean and wipe the toilet, wash your hands, and remove whatever you have on the door. Clean the window if you have to and spray the room with air freshener if you have any or just leave the door open.

Dental Hygiene

When you brush your teeth, always try to keep the toothpaste in your mouth and not slobbering all over the sink and your hand. Have the water running, and when you are ready to expectorate (spit it out), be sure you spit out the toothpaste into the toilet, period! No questions please. Rinse your mouth, and again, spit it into the toilet. Rinse your brush and clean your hands. When finished, wipe the sink dry and wipe down the toilet. Do this, and life in a three-man cell will go by quickly and without incident. (I never found a logical explanation as to why one must spit in the toilet. I was in a cell with two white guys who were OK with using the sink the way intended, and we spat out into the sink every time we brushed our teeth, and none of us came down with any type of disease or illness. These processes of using the toilet while brushing are inane, but do it at first until you know your cellys better. Just be sure to wipe the sink down real good after spitting in it.)

Clean as You Go

You will wash your hands and face a lot in prison. When you use your sink in your cell, try to keep the water in the sink, and if any water gets on the floor, be sure to wipe it up. You will find that toilet tissue has many uses in prison besides just wiping your ass. Clean as you go (isn't that a McDonald's thing?), and all will be OK. The same goes for when you are shaving. Be sure you clean everything when you are finished, and wipe it all down dry.

Follow the Same Routine Every Day

Waking up in the morning presents a huge problem when living in a three-man cell because you need to coordinate who is going to get up first, second, and last. This order is especially followed when in a cell with black inmates. White guys could care less, but the black inmates feel they need to be in control of everyone and everything. If you have black cell mates, go with the flow.

Depending on the jobs you each have, it may be necessary for someone to get up ahead of the others, and part of the problem is solved right there. Besides getting up to pee in the middle of the night or early morning, when one can't help but get up, you **will need** to work out a schedule for getting up, getting dressed, and getting out of the cell so that the next guy can follow suit until all three of you are through. If you need to take a shit, hold it in until all three of you are done getting ready for the day, unless you really need to go. If you are one who must take a crap every morning, be sure you are the last man to get ready so that when you are finished getting dressed, you can use the toilet right away for your cellys are already out of the cell. Only kick them out or ask them to leave when it is absolutely necessary. Always be aware of your cell mate's needs and always try to know what their idiosyncrasies are.

Outside the Cell

You have woken up, brushed your teeth, gone to the bathroom, and gotten yourself dressed. You are now out of the cell and still in the unit. In the morning, it is always a good thing to remain as quiet as possible until everyone is up and out of their cells. Unfortunately, there are some men that do not care about others and what time of the day it is, and they are always noisy in what they do or loud in what they have to say. Put up with it, but do not become a part of it. Do not become one of the animals.

If you are still in the unit, check the callout sheet, read a book, write a letter, or watch TV if any are turned on.

Once you are out and about on the compound, it just takes common sense to be able to get along with everyone else and not get in anyone's face. Be sure to keep a safe distance from other inmates and never walk too close to one from behind. If an inmate feels he is being intimidated, he will act accordingly, and in many instances, you will not know when and where he will retaliate if he feels you invaded his space.

O Rah

No, it is not a cheer or something from the marines. Those are two words you will hear over and over again every day you are down. O rah is the response that you will receive from almost every black inmate if you greet him on the compound. You say how are you doing? O rah. Hey, Jackson! O rah. What's going on? O rah. O rah is the lazy man's all right. Most black inmates will not dignify a response properly and always just say o rah to whatever is directed at them while passing on the compound. After a while, you will no longer do the decent or proper thing and greet someone as he walks by for he will just say o rah. It gets old after a while, and it is just like knocking on the table when you sit down or get up in the mess hall. No one knows how or where the custom began. I personally think it is just men being lazy and that is the easiest thing to say and it answers to anything, even if you don't understand the initial greeting.

Fun in the Dining Hall

This is where you will really have to be on your toes and best behavior for many inmates do not like having their meals or food compromised in any way, and you will find that there are many ways in which to do it, and you will not even realize you are doing it in some instances.

It can be during any meal, breakfast, lunch, or dinner—it does not matter; whatever you do, do not ever reach over another man's tray, food, or drink. It is not like at home when you are constantly reaching across another's plate to get some extra mashed potatoes or another helping of pasta. In prison, it is a huge no-no. You will get stares, men getting in your face, and possibly into a fight for just reaching over another man's food. I do not know any simpler way to put it. **DO NOT REACH OVER ANOTHER MAN'S FOOD, TRAY, OR DRINK.**

When you are in line to get your meal, you may see the guy ahead of you getting an extra piece of chicken, a second scoop of vegetables, or additional dessert. There is always a reason as to why this guy is getting more food. He may be the line server's celly or has done something for the guy and this is his way of getting paid. Heck, he may just be a homey. Whatever the reason is, do not expect to get the same treatment unless you too know the server or are owed something from him. Just do not make a stink about it. Do not ever get in the server's face and say something dumb like "Hey, man, I'll take a second piece of chicken too, just like you gave that guy" because that is what is called fronting the guy, and you do not front anyone in prison. It is like calling someone out for a fight. Once you are down long enough, you will know enough people in food service, where you will be able to get a few perks every so often.

The best way to get more food and better food is to work in food service. In most prisons, the food-service workers get fed real well at short line. The hours suck, but if you like to eat and eat good, then food service is the place for you. The job is usually six to eight hours a day, and one positive aspect of working there is that your time goes quicker.

Over time, you will see what you can and what you should not do in prison. Inmates have their own code of ethics and make up a lot of their own rules. Once you are aware of them, the better off you will be. If you want to be a rogue inmate and live by your own rules, have fun, for life in the joint will be a living hell. In prison, you need to do two things: adapt and be patient. Do those two things, and life will be much easier for you and everyone you come in contact with.

That was the prisoner's code of ethics or etiquette in prison. Chose to go by it or not—just watch out if you do not.

The next few chapters will tell you about services offered at each prison. The extent of what is offered varies greatly from one location to the other.

SERVICES AND PROGRAMS

SERVICES AND PROGRAMS

You will find all of the following in your Admissions and Orientation Handbook (Appendix B). What the handbook says and what actually happens are open for interpretation. Remember, you are dealing with the Federal Government and you know how politicians operate: They say or promise something and rarely deliver. Enough said.

Inmate Concerns and Grievances

At some point during your stay in prison, you will have a problem that will need to be addressed by someone in the administration. Many times, these issues can be answered directly by the person you want to hear it, during main line. At least one or two times per week, the prison administrators make their presence known at lunchtime and are there to answer any questions or concerns that you may have. If you feel that your issue(s) had not been addressed or handled properly or the answer was not what you had hoped to hear, you may file a grievance with the institution you are in. If you still are not satisfied with the answer, you may appeal to higher authorities outside your prison.

The first step is to personally speak with an administrator.

If that does not work, your next step is to file a **BP-148** or what is widely known as a cop-out. Most cop-outs are usually responded to within a few weeks' time, but there is no limit on when a cop-out is to be responded to.

If the cop-out does not yield results, the next step you must take is to fill out a **BP-229(13)**. You will hear people speaking about filling out a BP-9, which is the same thing. You can ask your counselor for a BP-9, and he or she will furnish you with the BP-229(13). A BP-9 is a blue form that is going to go directly to the warden of your facility, and the name of this form is Request for Administrative Remedy.

If you are not happy with how the Warden responded to your concern or grievance, your next plan of action is to file a **BP-230(13)** or better known as a BP-10. This is a yellow form that will be sent directly to the regional administrator, and it must be filed within thirty days of the date that your BP-9 was received by the warden. Be careful to check the dates because in many instances, by the time you receive your BP-9 back, you will have less than thirty days to respond. There have been times when counselors held the responses back and inmates had less than one week to get a BP-10 out in the mail. (This also goes for when responding to BP-10s and BP-11s.)

Still not satisfied with what the Region has to say? You have one last chance to be heard, and that is by the Central Office in Washington, DC. This is a pink form, and you guessed it, it is called a BP-11. (**BP-231[13]**). Again, be sure to file this form within the prescribed time window, or it will be returned, and your appeal will be lost.

In addition to each BP form, be sure to attach any necessary exhibits or attachments and see to it that the right number of copies is sent with it. In most cases, you should refer to Program Statement 1330.13 to see how many copies are to accompany each different BP, for the quantities differ with each one.

Good luck, because in most cases, your efforts will be futile. But like the saying goes, "Every once in a great while, even a blind squirrel finds an acorn."

Program Reviews

Every 6 months (180 days), you will meet with your unit team to go over your progress at your current prison. Once you are within 1 year from being released, your program reviews will be every 3 months (90 days).

At these meetings, you are to make requests that will affect how you will live for the next 6 months. You will discuss halfway house options, transfers, job changes, and whatever you feel is pertinent to yourself being safe and secure during your stay in prison. You will find that for every one case manager that actually shows some interest in you, that there will be four or five that do not care whatsoever. How well you get along at your current prison has a lot to do with your unit team and how well they work with you and you, them. Unfortunately, most do not work with you.

Education

At A&O, you will fill out a form that will tell the Education Department what highest grade level in school you completed. If you did not graduate from high school, it is now mandatory in the federal prison system that inmates will not be released until they attain their GED.

All prisons offer some sort of education program, whereas some more than others. While I was at Jesup FSL, education was virtually nonexistent. Most of the courses were taught by inmates that really did not care, and in some cases, they would sign in their homeys so that those so-called students would get their learning certificates for that course without even attending a class. At one time, Jesup offered crafts, woodworking, and computer courses, but those are long gone.

At Miami FCI, it is a whole different ball game. The Education Department there is extensive. In addition to the Education Department, they have a career training center that helps get inmates ready for work outside once released. By the time I was released in the Spring of 2010, the career training center was just about fully up and running, but there were some things that were not available to inmates yet.

Many prisons have invested in the Rosetta Stone Foreign Language Program, where any inmate can choose to learn a new language if he or she so desires.

There are computer courses that prepare inmates for the business world as well as teach them keyboarding and basic computer applications. At Miami, you can also take drafting, blueprint reading, and AutoCAD classes if you have a thing for engineering or construction.

At most FCIs, you will find education departments just as good as the one at Miami.

All education departments have a leisure library and a law library. Some are combined and share the same space. There is also a media lab, were you can check out daily newspapers, magazines, and typewriters. You will find legal forms to use if you are working on a case or need to request something from a government entity. You can also utilize the leisure library's interlibrary loan system, where you can request books from outside sources (local libraries). Once you receive your loaner book, you will have thirty days in which to read or gather information from it before it has to be returned.

Medical and Dental

While all prisons have health services, do not expect the same medical and dental care that you had received while you were living on the outside. Unless you have some debilitating health issues, the health services will be at a minimum. If you enter prison with some serious issues, you will be put on a chronic-care program, where you will be seen by the medical staff every three months instead of on an as-necessary basis.

If you do have to go seek medical attention, be prepared to wait for hours and sometimes not even be seen on the day you were called out to medical. Patience is the key, unless you are really ill and need immediate medical attention. If that is the case, sometimes, one must draw attention to themselves so that the medical staff takes notice. Use your imagination on that one.

Dental problems? If one has most of his/her teeth and the dental staff can see that you have good dental hygiene, they will do their best to treat your problems. On the other hand, if one has bad teeth and poor dental hygiene, in many cases, the dental staff will just go ahead and remove the problem teeth instead of trying to save them. I recommend brushing your teeth a few times a day and flossing often. It is a good time to start, unless you are looking at getting dentures in the future.

Back to medical issues. If you feel you need to see the doctor, you will need to go to sick call and get an appointment. If you are not a chronic-care patient or not being seen for an ongoing issue, your inmate account will be (debited) charged $2. If you do not have the funds in your account, it will be taken out when you do.

As far as emergency treatment goes, just hope that you will never need it. While at Jesup, I have seen men being taken from their housing units in blankets, carried by five or six inmates because the guards on duty did not know how to properly use the gurneys available. Another instance, the guard did not know how to raise the gurney, so he pushed the inmate to medical with his feet. Pushing him a few feet until he rolled to a stop and continuing that way until he made it to the medical office.

A fellow inmate of mine was diagnosed with a hernia and was told that since it was not life threatening that it would be months before the medical staff could even refer him for surgery. After four months, he was having circulation problems in his right leg, and his leg was blowing up like a balloon. Finally, medical relented and scheduled him for surgery. He was sent across the street to the medium compound, where he was to get X-rays and preadmission tests done. It was at this time they found out that he did not have a hernia but, instead, a melanoma the size of an orange. He had cancer! For the next week, he was treated like royalty by everyone from the warden to the lowest corrections officer on the compound. Can you say lawsuit? Jesup got rid of the problem by shipping him to Butner, North Carolina, where he could be taken care of the right way. I just hope that he made it through and is doing OK. If you are worried that a diagnosis may be incorrect, it is tough getting a second opinion in prison. Good luck.

You can get eyeglasses while in prison, but it takes a few months before you will be seen by the optometrist. Once you do see him/her, they will order you glasses that are made at some UNICOR. Be prepared to have an ill-fitting pair of Buddy Holly glasses for the duration in prison unless you can have a pair sent in from the outside. To get a pair sent in from home, you must go through R&D to do it, and they have very stringent regulations. You may as well let the government pay for your glasses if you don't mind looking funny.

Religious Services

Every prison has men and women from just about every religious denomination, and each prison does its best to accommodate each one. There is a chapel at each institution, and that chapel serves host to almost every religion.

There is a chaplain available most times of the day to see to those requiring pastoral care, counseling, and assistance with emergency notices.

Worship notices are posted throughout the compounds and also posted on the chapel bulletin boards.

Inmates can request a common-fare religious diet that must be approved by the chaplain.

Telephones

Phone calls cost $0.23 per minute, which comes to $3.45 every time you make a fifteen-minute phone call. All calls are limited to fifteen minutes each, and once you make a call for any duration of time, you will not be allowed to make another call for one-half hour. The $3.45 price is for long-distance calls. Local calls are only for the area code in which your prison is located in. Local calls only cost $0.06 per minute or $0.90 per call.

What many inmates do is ask their loved ones or friends that they communicate with a lot to purchase a mobile phone with the area code of the city where their prison is located. That way, the calls would be much cheaper. Just do not call your friends and family so many times that they get sick of you. I have seen that happen. Be careful.

TRU-LINCS

Tru-Lincs is the inmate e-mail system and is now fully up and running.

Every housing unit has at least four Tru-Lincs computer terminals for inmates to use to e-mail family and friends. While that number may not sound like a lot, there is usually never a wait to go online. Tru-Lincs is available to most inmates yet is restricted to those who are serving time for a computer-generated crime or those serving time for a sex offense. While these inmates are excluded from using the services, they can still put in a request to have their case reviewed, and in some instances, these excluded inmates may have their e-mail privileges restored.

The cost of using the e-mail system is $0.05 per minute. It is cheaper than making a phone call unless the call is local. Whereas a fifteen-minute phone call costs $3.45, you can go online for thirty minutes for only $1.50. I used the e-mail more than I used the phone, but it is a good thing to call your loved ones and friends just to hear their voices every now and then.

You will not be able to send or receive pictures or attachments with this system for it is designed strictly for e-mails only.

There is about a two-hour delay from when you send an e-mail to when it is received on the other end, so do not expect immediate replies from those you send e-mails to. All outgoing e-mail has to be screened before it can go to its destination address.

Inmate Deposit Fund Account

Inmate funds are kept in an inmate deposit account that is established in your name once you are a ward of the BOP. These monies follow you from institution to institution and can be accessed at any time for commissary, family support, or other approved purposes, like subscribing to magazines, newspapers, and book purchases. You can also send money to your lawyer, friends, or family.

You may also access your account to put money into your phone account or purchase minutes to be used on Tru-Lincs.

If you need to have funds sent to you while you are incarcerated, have people send money to

Federal Bureau of Prisons
(Inmate name)
(Inmate's registration number)
PO Box 474701
Des Moines, Iowa 50947-0001

DO NOT have your people use nicknames, or you will not get your money. If having money sent, be sure that it is in the form of a United States postal money order or a Western Union money order. Cash and personal checks will not be accepted. Be sure that whoever sends you funds, they put their return address on the mailing envelope so that if there is a problem, they can get their money returned.

If your people decide that they want to use Western Union, they can stop at any WU counter with cash, debit card, or credit card or go online using a debit or credit card. Using Western Union is much quicker, and inmates will see money posted to their accounts usually within two hours after the transaction was completed. Funds put in after 9:00 p.m. will not clear until the opening of business on the next day, which is usually around 9:00 a.m.

Funds sent to the lockbox in Des Moines usually take from seven to fourteen days to clear.

When using Western Union Quick Collect, the following information must be provided:

Inmate registration number

Inmate name

City code: FBOP

State code: DC

The information for Western Union (city and state codes) pertains to everywhere in the United States.

There are some fees involved when using Western Union, but I feel it is worth the few extra dollars to get the funds into your account quicker.

WU can also be accessed by telephone. Be sure your people provide the operator with the information provided above.

Recreation

Every prison has a recreation (rec) yard that can be accessed by all inmates at any time of the day while the compound is opened and you are not on your work detail. In the Fed, it is not like what you see on TV where it looks like just a dirt-and-gravel field with a basketball hoop hanging from a phone pole.

At Miami FCI, there are indoor and outdoor basketball courts, two boccie courts, a running and walking track, a softball field, a soccer field, two racquetball courts, a beach-volleyball court, a three-on-three soccer court, pool tables, Ping-Pong, board games, and of course, a weight pile.

Inside the rec building, there are rooms dedicated to crafts, such as music, art, pottery, and leather craft.

You will also find the inmate barber shop in this building.

Not all prisons have what I mentioned above. Some may have all this and more while some may have less or much less.

Commissary

While in prison, you will need to go shopping. Every prison has its own inmate store where inmates can shop for just about anything they need from sundry items to medical supplies. The prisons set the prices, so be prepared to pay more than you would at a local convenience store. The sad thing is that convenience-store prices are the highest prices out there. You are not getting any type of break because you are in prison. Just the reverse—they rape you with the high prices because they know you will pay it if you have the funds. Example, eight ounces of Philadelphia brand cream cheese costs $1.49 in a convenience store and $2.50 in prison. A six-pack of Yoo-hoo cans costs almost $6. Come on!

You are allowed to spend up to $290 per month and, in some institutions, only $145 every two weeks. Each time you are to shop, you must fill out a commissary list (See Appendix A) and have it ready when your number is called.

Laundry

Each housing unit has at least two washing machines and two dryers for at least 150 inmates per housing unit. You can purchase a laundry card at commissary that will allow you 5 washes and 5 dries, which works out to a little under $1 each. You have to put your laundry in line and monitor it very closely. Some days, you can get right in and right out, and other days, it will take hours to get a load cleaned and dried. Some inmates overload the machines with blankets and sheets, and the machines break down often.

You can pay someone to do your laundry. You will have to supply him/her with your card and detergent.

If you do your laundry in the unit, the main benefit is that you are only washing your clothes in one machine at one time and using good detergent. Commissary sells Tide with bleach for about $8 for twenty-four loads or Trend for about $3. You can use a dryer sheet to make your clothes smell fresh as well. You will notice your T-shirts and whites remain white much longer than if you used the prison laundry facility.

Prison laundry washes clothes at least three times a week and bed linens once a week. They use commercial machines, so your clothes are washed with other inmates' clothes as well. You are issued a net bag in which to store your soiled clothing, and the entire net bag with clothes in it gets washed as one. They use little if any detergent, and many times, your clothes are damp or wet when you pick them up. If you happen to have your clothes in with clothes of those that may have been in the rec yard, playing softball on the red clay, your whites will come back discolored. Eventually, you will call your whites browns after a few weeks at the prison laundry. You will also find the natty, twirled hair of those with dreadlocks that get caught in your bag. Live with it or take the time to do your laundry in the unit. The wait time is worth it.

Visits

Visits usually go from Thursday to Sunday or Friday to Monday and can last for up to seven hours, depending on how crowded your institution's visitation room is on the day of your visit. Once you have friends and family on your visitation list that must be submitted to your counselor, they can go and visit you, and you will be able to physically sit with them without having to deal with a screen or a glass partition between you and your guests. As long as you do not get carried away, a kiss and a hug are allowed.

You must wear your prison-issued khakis and work shoes to visitations. Some places allow inmates to wear their sneakers or tennis shoes, but many do not.

FAMILY AND FRIENDS = SUPPORT

Before I venture in to the not-so-legal ways to survive in prison, there is one thing that I must mention and which I have not touched on wholly as of yet, and that is the support you need from family and friends.

These two groups of people are the most important things that one will need to navigate their way through the prison system. I really do not have to go on about their importance for everyone knows that family and friends make up the core support group in any environment.

Once you are designated for a prison, you would only hope that you will not be too far away from home. In most cases, the courts will try to sentence you to a prison that is located no more than five hundred miles from where you last resided. Sometimes, this does not happen, and you end up being so far away that visits will be few and far between. The only advice that I can give you is that you remain problem-free for eighteen months, and then you will be qualified to put in for a transfer to a prison closer to your home or family.

It is best not to make enemies of your family and friends because they will be your main arena of support for the duration of your time behind the razor wire. It will be these people that send you monetary support as well, so you do not want to go and burn too many bridges by making yourself a nuisance to anyone.

At first, many of your friends and some of your family members will distance themselves from you and you will just have to let time heal those wounds. Remember that it was your bad choice and subsequent actions that caused shame and embarrassment to many of those that were close to you, and they will need time to come back to you. You cannot force anyone to forgive you or help you, so it is in your best interest to not treat those you love badly.

Always try to call these people that are on your support team at least once a month or reach out to them through Tru-Lincs or by mail. If they cannot help you out financially, be glad that you have them in your corner anyway. They may be able to help you out somewhere down the line, and while incarcerated, you want all the friends that you can get. Believe me; once you are down for a few months, it always is a great thing to hear family members' or friends' voices on the phone or to receive a piece of mail from one of them regularly.

THE NOT-SO-LEGAL WAYS
TO SURVIVE IN PRISON

Earlier in the book, I wrote how some people had their hustle and that inmates should try to avoid taking part in one if they possibly could. Unfortunately, we are dealing with reality, and not everyone going to prison has the people or the means on the outside to support them on the inside.

I was lucky to have family that stood by me every inch of the way and saw to it that my necessities were taken care of out of their own pockets.

I have seen firsthand, how many inmates made commissary money and spending "money" in the form of USPS postage stamps. In prison, two $0.49 stamps equal $1 and one book of stamps is equal to $10. Inmates discount the amount 30% when one spends stamps to purchase items in commissary or from other inmates. So, $30 in prison cash will get you $21 in commissary or items from other prisoners. That is the way the system works in the Fed.

I mentioned in a previous chapter that "the animals run the zoo" and that is very much evidenced by the following, so called, inmate initiated jobs. While these jobs are frowned upon by the prison staff, they have been in place long before I arrived in 2005 and will go on long after my release, back in 2010. They are ingrained in the prison culture.

While being behind the razor wire is a bad and sad situation to be in, it is an everyday occurrence in prison where rules are being broken.

They are tolerated by the Warden, his or her staff, and the guards because if they allow the prisoners to get away with certain things, then everyday operations runs a lot smoother for everyone. It is when a prisoner disrespects a guard or guards by, for example, not removing poker chips from the table as a guard approaches, or walking right by a guard with a box of chicken from the kitchen, etc., that a game is shut down or a prisoner is sent to The Hole for theft.

I do not condone, nor do I recommend any of these jobs to anyone reading this book, but feel they must be mentioned, for there are some men and women who will feel the need to possibly engage in such an endeavor due to the lack of support from friends and family on the outside. Be advised, that if an inmate tries his or her hand at one of these jobs, he or she will eventually get caught and will do time in the facility's Special Housing Unit (SHU) or what is known as "The Hole," Solitary confinement. Inmates will spend at least 15 days in The Hole.

While in the SHU, or The Hole, inmates are locked down 24/7 and let out of the cell for 1 hour a day for recreation, which is walking around in walled in area, nothing more. They are allowed 1 phone call a week and maybe 3 showers a week if the guards like that inmate. In addition to being locked down 24/7, inmates stand the chance (a very good chance) to lose good time accrued or a portion of it, thus extending their sentence. If a prisoner had the luxury of being in a 2 man cell, once released from The Hole, they will be relegated back to a 3 man with no chance of getting back in to a 2 man.

Following is the list of sanctions that are imposed when inmates are caught participating in these activities:

A. Recommend parole date rescission or retardation.
B. Forfeit earned statutory good time fo non-vested good conduct up to 25% or up to 30 days, whichever is less, and/or terminate or disallow extra good time (an extra good conduct time sanction may not be suspended).
C. Disciplinary Transfer (recommend).

D. Disciplinary segregation (up to 15 days, maybe more).

E. Make monetary restitution.

F. Withhold statutory good time.

G. Loss of privileges: commissary, movies, recreation, etc.

H. Change housing (quarters).

I. Remove from program and/or group activity.

J. Loss of job.

K. Impound inmate's personal property. [This one really hurts inmates.]

L. Confiscate contraband.

M. Restrict to quarters.

N. Extra duty.

Those inmates who even think about partaking in one or more of these jobs will want to ask themselves if it is worth the problems that will arise when they eventually get caught.

Listed below are the many ways in which I have seen inmates make "prison money:"

- Food-service mule
- Food-service worker
- Store man
- Bookmaker
- Skin Lottery
- Cigarettes
- Pot and cocaine
- Laundry and cleaning services
- Poker

Due to restrictions put on me by my publisher, there are certain jobs I cannot elaborate on because it goes against their policy that the author (me), "...further represent that the Work does not contain illegal, unlawful or objectionable material..." While I do not agree with their decision to censor part of my book, I must abide by their decision.

If you purchased this book because you are looking at going to prison or know someone who may be going, I cannot tell you to look in to these types of "jobs" for they are considered illegal by the prisons standards, but are practiced daily, nonetheless.

If you bought this book because you are curious of what goes on in Federal Prisons, then you may want to read this chapter for the entertainment value and see what extremes some inmates go to in order to make commissary or prison money.

Anyone wishing the uncensored chapter "The Not-So-Legal Ways to Survive in Prison" can send an e-mail to the author and it will be sent (USPS) to you at no charge. Or, if you prefer, the chapter can be transmitted to you via e-mail. Just be sure to state that in the request.

All you have to do is go to the book website, www.itsonlyhell.com and go to the "CONTACT THE AUTHOR" tab. Be sure to enter all the necessary fields. In the message section, be sure to state if you want it mailed to you or e-mailed. If you do want the chapter mailed to you, please don't forget to put the mailing address in the message field.

Please allow 1-2 weeks for your request to be filled.

The contents of the censored chapter:

Food Service Mule:

Due to publisher terms, this sub chapter cannot be included in this book. Feel free to write the author and the chapter, in its entirety, will be mailed to you FREE.

Food Service Worker:

Due to publisher terms, this sub chapter cannot be included in this book. Feel free to write the author and the chapter, in its entirety, will be mailed to you FREE.

Store Man:

Due to publisher terms, this sub chapter cannot be included in this book. Feel free to write the author and the chapter, in its entirety, will be mailed to you FREE.

Bookmaker:

Due to publisher terms, this sub chapter cannot be included in this book. Feel free to write the author and the chapter, in its entirety, will be mailed to you FREE.

Skin (porn) Lottery:

Due to publisher terms, this sub chapter cannot be included in this book. Feel free to write the author and the chapter, in its entirety, will be mailed to you FREE.

Cigarettes:

Due to publisher terms, this sub chapter cannot be included in this book. Feel free to write the author and the chapter, in its entirety, will be mailed to you FREE.

Pot and cocaine:

Due to publisher terms, this sub chapter cannot be included in this book. Feel free to write the author and the chapter, in its entirety, will be mailed to you FREE.

Laundry and Cleaning Services:

There are inmates that do not mind waiting around for loads of laundry to wash and dry and it is these people that have no problem running a laundry service.

Most housing units only have 2 washing machines and 2 dryers (if all are working) to service upward of 150 inmates per unit.

Many inmates take their clothes to the institution laundry, but they have to worry about cleanliness, for their laundry is washed in a net bag along with the net bags of other inmates at the same time in commercial washing machines that use barely any soap or laundry detergent. The bags are washed mostly with warm water.

When an inmate's laundry is picked up, it has hair and dirt from other inmates' dirty laundry staining and sticking out of their own. Not good.

If inmates do their own laundry in the unit, the wait sometimes can be two or three hours or more on certain days. If an inmate's time is worth $10 in commissary each month, then it is worth it to invest in a laundry man/service.

The laundry man is responsible for picking up, washing, drying, folding and returning the laundry to each customer/inmate paying for the service each day. In most cases, the laundry man has the inmate whose laundry they are doing, purchase the detergent and leave it with them. If that inmate feels uncomfortable leaving a box of detergent with the laundry man (I would not leave it) the inmate will put the desired amount of powdered detergent in a sock and knot the sock closed. He will do that for each load he expects to be done. Usually, no more than 2. It is the laundry man's responsibility to find the socks and use the detergent accordingly.

In most prisons it costs $1.00 per load (as of 2010) to wash and to dry. That cost is covered by the inmate, and either he can give the laundry man his laundry card with the money prepaid on it or it can be worked in to the cost of doing business and the laundry man will use his own card.

Every 2 weeks, inmates must wash their sheets and blankets, and that works out to an additional $1 to $1.50. If the inmate is using his laundry card, he must make sure there is at least $8.00 on it each month.

When an inmate decides that he or she wants to be a laundry person, they can accumulate as many clients as they wish. This job is very time consuming, but in prison, inmates have nothing but time. If a prisoner can get about 15 clients, that will work out to better than $150 in commissary each month, and this job is one that is never really given any attention to by the guards or staff. How do they know who's laundry is being done?

Some inmates also clean cells and mop and wax the floors in cells for $10 a month, too. They clean the cell two times per week and wax the floors two times per month.

Two Tough Jobs to Get

If by chance an inmate happened to land a job working in the institution laundry or in the Commissary, they can make some serious money/commissary from these 2 positions.

In the laundry facility, inmate workers can wash and fold other inmates laundry on an individual basis instead of with numerous other net bags that almost guarantee not getting completely clean. In most instances the supervisor is not around and laundry inmates can use hot water and good detergent, so the clients know their things are being cleaned.

The inmate will pick up his laundry at the designated time with everyone else, but his clothes are washed and folded. The nice thing about doing laundry this way is that the clothes are removed from the net bag and guaranteed complete wash coverage in the washer and dryer. The clothes are also washed on an individual basis, not with those of other inmates. Inmates are usually charged from $5 to $10 a month for this service.

If an inmate has a job in the Commissary, they can take client commissary lists to work with them. When the worker spots the client outside waiting to shop, he will take that clients list and fill the order for them without them having to wait in line. Sometimes, the wait is substantial, and the inmate may miss the hourly move and have to wait until the next move 50 minutes later. This way, inmates are guaranteed to make the first compound move. The worse thing is having to wait almost an hour for the compound to re-open, especially if you have ice cream.

The method of payment for this service is simple. The commissary worker just adds an item or two to the clients order and picks up those items up after the shift is over. He must go to the other inmates unit, and has to be careful because technically you are not allowed in units other than your own. Guards rarely enforce that restriction, though. The pay usually works out to $2 an order. If an inmate fills 10 orders a day, that person makes about $20 in commissary. Works out to about $80 to $100 a week. Not bad.

The two positions just mentioned are hard to come by, and the inmates that get these positions are ones that cozy up to the guards or CO running those jobs. That's is where it pays to be a kiss ass, but there can be a fine line between being a kiss ass and a snitch. Inmates have to be careful.

WHEN ALL ELSE FAILS

For the most part, during my tenure in federal prison, I tried to stay away from things and activities that would get me into trouble. I cannot say that I was a saint, and I will confess that I did try my hand at the poker table and held my own but ultimately lost as time went on. I employed an inmate (a guy that did not have much support from the outside) to wash my clothes each week for $10 a month. It made me feel good that I could help another human being who was not as fortunate as me. On occasion, I did take some things from food service for my own consumption even though I knew it was wrong.

The majority of my time was spent working in food service and doing the right thing while on the job. When not working, I found legal activities to keep me occupied. I learned how to speak Spanish (began working with Rosetta Stone) and how to correctly keyboard (type) as evidenced by this book in its rough draft form. I took business courses that can help me as I remain free, and I signed up to watch a movie that took me out of touch with the prison environment for about two hours each week.

Besides wanting to get back to see my children and resume a freedom of living on the outside again, what really kept me going and kept me from doing something unthinkable was my faith in God. I tried my hardest to renew my relationship with Jesus Christ and knew that I was rewarded for my faith and praise of God in seeing how I survived without a scratch for over four and a half years.

While at the Union City Jail in Georgia, while working on my case, I was assaulted once by an inmate who had recently been removed from his meds. Nothing after that though.

God has taken care of me, without a doubt, and I know for a fact that it was he who had my back the whole time that I was down.

In 2009, I did have a minor setback, an emotional breakdown that was attributed to situational depression. Duh! I was in prison!

Soon after that, God gave me back my son, Michael, after not communicating with me for almost three years.

Through my talking with God and my devout faith in Jesus, I was able to overcome the adversity of being locked up in a cage for over four years and leave prison a better person.

I will not lie and say every day was good. There were times when my faith wavered and that I just wanted to give up. It was at these times when I would speak to God and ask him to give me the strength to persevere through the rough times.

There were times when I found myself talking out loud to Jesus, and I never did that on the outside except in church. Other men would hear me, and it did not bother me in the least. I am not the best Christian on this planet, but my belief in God made for a much better stay in prison.

DO NOT abandon God, Jesus, or whomever you pray to, be it Allah, Mohammed, Buddha, or Jehovah. Keep your faith strong, and you will get through this. A lot has to do with how you carry yourself as well as witness to others your faith. I have not gotten to the point where I can totally give of myself to the Lord, so I must endure hardships along the way and experience days that I wish would never happen.

I do know this—I have been forgiven by God my transgression that put me here and know there is a place waiting for me at his side. If my faith were stronger, there would be no need for the information in this book. We are not perfect, and we are far from perfect with our god, so I feel this book is necessary for all of us.

Good luck, and do not make any dumb choices. You already did that, and that is why you are reading this book.

GLOSSARY

AW—Associate warden.

BET—Black entertainment television. Don't worry, you'll find it everywhere.

Boo Game—Verbal threats that never end up with physical contact, most of the time, just a lot of yelling and chest-thumping.

BOP or B.O.P.—Bureau of Prisons.

BP 9, 10, or 11—Forms BP-229(13), BP-230(13), and BP-231(13) used by inmates to remedy problems encountered in prison. First starts with the warden and then to the region and, finally, with general counsel in Washington, DC.

Bus clothes—Institution clothing issued when an inmate is transferred between prisons.

Callout sheet—Form usually found in each housing unit that shows which inmates have appointments for that day. You must show up for the appointment, or disciplinary action can be taken against you.

Case manager—Person on your unit team responsible for monitoring your progress while at each prison you are at. This person is also responsible for setting up your halfway house and release. You usually will have to stay on top of these people for some do a half-assed job.

Cash—$1.00 stamps or two $0.49 stamps. A book of $0.49 stamps is equal to $10.00 even though it only costs $9.80.

CO or C.O.—Corrections officer or compound officer.

Commissary—Facility store in which food, health, grooming items, clothes, and sundries can be purchased using inmate monetary funds.

Con Air—The white unmarked 727 that the Fed uses to transport prisoners when it is too far to transport them by bus or van.

Contraband—Anything that is not issued to you by the BOP and found in your living quarters or in your possession.

Cop-out—Form BP-148 that is a written request to a staff member or an administrator.

Documentation—Usually a Presentence Investigation Report (PSI) or your sentence calculation form. These forms both show your charges, and in some places, you are asked to present one of these forms to show what you are in prison for and, in most cases, to see if you are a sex offender or not. It is up to you if you want to present these or not, for it is no one's business but your own and the BOP's as to why you are in prison.

Drop paper—When one sends a cop-out to staff telling on another inmate or inmates. Snitching.

Ear hustle—Listening in on another's conversation not intended for you to hear.

Eye hustle—Checking out another's cell or living quarters for something to take or steal. Reading over one's shoulder or reading another person's mail or documentation without their consent.

Finger fuck—Touching or taking another inmate's personal property or anything that does not belong to you, period.

Fronting—The easiest way to put it, snitching on someone in their presence.

Homeys—Your closest prison associates.

Lower- or bottom-bunk pass—A medical exemption that makes it mandatory for an inmate to be issued a lower bunk throughout his tenure in the BOP. Be sure to tell the medical staff everything that is wrong with you. Also, it is a good thing to let them know how old you are, especially if you are over fifty. I have seen men in their sixties and seventies in top bunks.

Main line—Chow line designated for the general population.

Mule—Inmate used by the thieves in food service to take stolen goods from the dining room and kitchen back to the units.

On the take—Taking bribes. A person that will do an illegal favor for another. This person is usually compensated monetarily—but in prison, sexual favors are not uncommon.

Pill line—Called right after breakfast and right before dinner when prescription drugs are distributed for daily intake and prescriptions are given out.

Pod—Another name for a jail or prison unit of cells, usually set apart from other pods. For example, C pod is where they house federal inmates in a county jail.

Police, five-oh, or the po po—Prison guards or corrections officers. Sometimes relating to prison administration or staff touring a unit.

"Put some water on it!"—Flush the fucking toilet! By the time someone says that to you, you have offended someone.

Short line—Meal provided for the kitchen help before main line.

Shot—Incident report filed against an inmate for violating a rule or regulation of the institution or BOP. This is usually filed by the staff member that witnesses the infraction.

Snitch—One who tells the staff or administration about illegal or illicit actions of another inmate or inmates.

Staged and staging area—Places in the kitchen and dish room that are used by the thieves to conceal the stolen goods until the mules can come and take them back to the units.

Standing count—In most prisons, there is a standing count at 4:00 p.m. every day and at 10:00 a.m. on weekends and holidays. It is just like it says, a standing count, meaning that you must be standing in your cell during this count, or directly outside it if instructed otherwise.

Store—Legally, it is the commissary. Otherwise, it is food, sundry, health, and clothing items sold in the unit for 50 percent over cost or on a two-for-three return.

Store man—Inmate who runs a store from his cell and/or lockers.

Tru-Lincs—The inmate electronic e-mail system that allows inmates to communicate with friends, family, business associates, etc.

UNICOR—Prison industry or another name for a legalized sweatshop.

Appendix A

Commissary sheet

FCI / FPC MIAMI COMMISSARY LIST

PUBLISHED MARCH 2013

FULL NAME (PRINT)	Shoes [Limit 1] Indicate Size by Style	Miscellaneous Items	REGISTER NUMBER
Stamps [Limit 20 First Class Stamps]	$75.10 Running	$5.85 Copy Card	**Shopper Information**
$0.46 Forever Stamp	$64.95 X-Trainer	$1.00 Photo Ticket	**[Check Only If Applies]**
$0.10 10¢ Stamp	$79.90 Basketball	[1 Photo](Limit 10)	___ First Time Shopper
$0.01 1¢ Stamp	$41.60 Reebok Classic	SPO Item#	___ Medical Items Only
$1.00 *$1 Stamp	$76.50 Work Boot		

Ice Cream [Limit 3 Total]

1.90 ¤ Vanilla Pint		1.90 ¤ Chocolate Chaos Pint		1.90 ¤ Butter Pecan Pint	
1.90 ¤ Cookies & Cream Pint		1.90 ¤ Banana Split Pint		1.90 ¤ Split Decision Pint	
1.40 ¤ Champ Vanilla Cone		0.95 ¤ Pineapple Bar		1.20 ¤ Big Neo Sandwich	
1.90 ¤ Orange Sherbet Pint					

Drinks [Limit 2 Packs Soda Total]

5.20 ¤ Diet Mountain Dew	2	5.20 ¤ Strawberry Crush	2	5.20 ¤ Sierra Mist Natural	2	5.20 ¤ Diet Pepsi	2
5.20 ¤ Pepsi Cola	2	5.20 ¤ Grape Crush	2	2.75 Instant Tea W/Lem. Fusion	2	2.05 ¤ Pineapple Drink Fusions	2
4.10 ¤ Powdered Milk	2	1.75 ¤ Lipton Tea Bags	2	0.90 Gatorade Lemon Lime	5	1.85 Hot Chocolate	2
1.85 ¤ Pink Lemonade	2	1.95 Gatorade Fruit Punch	3	1.20 ¤ Lemon Berry Mix	2	1.00 ¤ Peach Mix	2
1.30 ¤ Hawaiian Punch Fruity	2	2.05 ¤ Tang Orange Drink Mix	2				
		1.30 Hawaiian Punch Blue Berry	2				

Nuts & Candies [Note Limits Next To Each Item]

2.75 ¤ Raw Trail Mix	3	3.10 ¤ Honey Roasted Peanuts	3	3.00 ¤ California Mix	3	3.00 ¤ Almonds	3
3.10 ¤ Deluxe Mixed Nuts	3	2.45 ¤ Salted Peanuts	10	1.10 ¤ Dove Dark Chocolate	10	1.00 ¤ M&M's W/Peanuts	10
1.00 ¤ Kit-Kat	10	1.00 ¤ Hershey's W/Almonds	10	0.95 ¤ Snickers	10	2.60 Tootsie Roll Pops Bag	2
1.45 ¤ S/F Tropical Candy Bag	3	0.65 Star Lite Mints Bag	5	0.60 Atomic Fireballs Bag	5	0.95 Certs 5 Flavor Roll	10
0.20 Chic-O-Stick Individual	10	0.80 Jolly Rancher's Bag	2	1.40 Peanut Clusters Bag	5	0.85 Skittles	10
0.85 Almond Joy	10						

Coffee Items [Note Limits Next To Each Item]

3.75 ¤ Splenda Sugar Substitute	1	2.20 ¤ Sugar Twins II	1	2.05 ¤ Sugar Cubes	1	1.60 ¤ Coffee Creamer	2
3.40 ¤ Colombian Coffee	2	3.40 ¤ Decaf. Colombian Coffee	2	7.25 ¤ Folgers Coffee	2	8.95 ¤ Decaf. Folgers Coffee	2
2.55 Boston Colombian Coffee	2						

Food Items [Note Limits Next To Each Item]

4.00 ¤ Honey Nut Scooters Cereal	2	4.85 ¤ Raisin Bran Cereal	2	4.15 ¤ Berry Colossal Cereal	2	2.50 ¤ Banana Nut Gran. Cereal	2
3.85 ¤ Cinnamon Toasters	2	2.55 ¤ Assorted Oatmeal Box	2	2.20 ¤ Plain Oatmeal	2	1.65 ¤ Balance Bar French Vanilla	10
1.65 ¤ Balance Bar Peanut butter	10	0.55 ¤ Butter Popcorn	10	0.55 ¤ Natural Popcorn	10	1.05 ¤ Macaroni & Cheese	10
0.95 ¤ Blueberry Pop-tarts	5	2.50 ¤ Choc Chip Granola Bar	2	2.50 ¤ Strawberry Fruit Bar	2	3.15 ¤ Akmak Crackers	2
5.00 ¤ Matzo Crackers	1	2.00 ¤ Cuban Crackers	2	3.95 ¤ Ritz Crackers	1	2.60 ¤ Low Salt Saltines	1
1.70 ¤ Honey Buns Box	2	2.15 ¤ Powder Donuts	2	1.70 ¤ Oatmeal Cream Pies Box	2	2.35 ¤ Iced Oatmeal Cookies	1
		0.80 ¤ Peanut Butter Cookies	2	0.80 ¤ Strawberry Cookies	2	0.85 ¤ Maria Cookies	2
2.85 ¤ Cheese Danish	2	2.85 ¤ Cinnamon Danish	2	1.75 ¤ Peanut Butter Wafers	2	2.35 ¤ Vanilla Wafers	2
0.50 ¤ Soft Oatmeal Raisin Cookies	5	0.50 ¤ Soft Choco. Chip Cookies	5	2.80 ¤ Velveeta Cheese Block	5	3.05 ¤ Wheat-Germ	1
2.80 ¤ Quaker Instant Grits Box	1	1.50 ¤ Soy Sauce	1	1.70 ¤ Chicken Bouillon	2	2.75 ¤ Creamy Peanut Butter	1

Item	Qty	Item	Qty	Item	Qty	Item	Qty
1.60 ¤ Goya Sazón	1	1.20 ¤ Green Olives	2	3.45 ¤ Wheat Thins Box	2	0.55 ¤ Bagels	10
1.15 ¤ Mustard	1	1.90 ¤ Ketchup	1	1.10 ¤ Dried Onion Flakes	1	1.35 ¤ Vegetable Flakes	2
3.15 ¤ Mrs. Dash Original	1	3.15 ¤ Mrs. Dash Spicy	1	1.50 ¤ Salt & Pepper Set.	1	2.05 ¤ Adobo Goya Seasoning	1
1.15 ¤ Mackerel Fillets	10	2.00 ¤ Whole Wheat Tortillas	5	2.25 ¤ Large Flour Tortilla	5	2.70 ¤ Pink Salmon	10
1.50 ¤ Chunky Light Tuna	10	1.40 ¤ Kippered Snack	10	1.95 ¤ Albacore Tuna	10	1.90 ¤ Pepperoni	10
2.00 ¤ Turkey Summer Sausage	10	1.95 ¤ Yellow Fin Tuna Steak	10	2.55 ¤ Chorizos	10	1.90 ¤ Hot & Spicy Beef Sausage	10
1.00 ¤ Turkey & Swiss Sticks	10	1.70 ¤ Beef Salami Sausage	10	1.65 ¤ Beef Summer Sausage	10	2.85 ¤ Pretzel Nuggets	5
1.80 ¤ Honey Turkey Bites	10	2.25 ¤ Halal Beef Sausage	10	3.70 ¤ Chicken Breast Pouch	10	0.80 ¤ Veggie Chilli W/Beans	5
3.45 ¤ Shredded Beef	10	1.60 ¤ Spam Single	10	4.15 ¤ Laughing Cow Cheese	2	1.00 ¤ Mozzarella Cheese	5
1.90 ¤ Refried Pinto Beans Bag	5	1.00 ¤ Hot Beef Deli Stick	10	0.95 ¤ Curry Powder Seasoning	1	1.70 ¤ Vietnam Hot Sauce	2
2.75 ¤ Black Bean Flakes Box	5	1.90 ¤ Jalapeno Pepper Wheels	2	3.30 ¤ Mayonnaise	1	2.00 ¤ Picante Sauce	1
2.95 ¤ Honey Bear	1	4.75 ¤ Olive Oil	1	0.75 ¤ Hot Sauce	2	1.65 ¤ Tortilla Chips	5
3.15 ¤ Strawberry Preserve	1	1.75 ¤ Sweet & Hot Sauce	2	2.40 ¤ Whole Enchilada Party Mix	5	1.75 ¤ Pork Rinds	5
1.55 ¤ Moon Lodge Barbecue	5	1.95 ¤ Cheetos Crunchy	5	1.85 ¤ Corn Chips	5	$1.90 Doritos Cool Ranch	5
1.30 ¤ Plantain Chips Original	5	1.30 ¤ Plantain Chips Garlic	5	1.95 ¤ Doritos Bite Size	5	1.55 ¤ Moon Lodge Sour Cream	5
2.25 ¤ Pringles Sour Cream	5	2.85 ¤ Chex Mix Original	5	1.60 ¤ Vegetable Chips	10	1.90 ¤ Sea Salt Chips	5
1.30 ¤ Brown Rice Instant	10	1.35 ¤ White Rice Instant	10	1.30 ¤ Black Bean Pouch	5	2.70 ¤ Chicken Noodle Soup	10
0.30 ¤ Hot Chili Ramen Soup	10	0.30 ¤ Shrimp Ramen Soup	10	0.30 ¤ Chick/Mushroom. Soup	10	0.50 ¤ Jalapeno-Cheddar Soup	10
0.55 ¤ Garlic Bulbs	2	0.50 ¤ Vegetable Soup Cup	10	0.55 ¤ Chicken Vegetable Soup Cup	10		

Miscellaneous Items [Limit 1 Each Unless Noted]

Item	Qty	Item	Qty	Item	Qty	Item	Qty
1.90 ¤ AA Batteries 4 Pack	2	1.90 ¤ AAA Batteries 4 Pack	2	2.20 ¤ C Batteries 2 Pack	2	1.50 ¤ Shower Cap	2
2.60 ¤ Shave Mirror W/Magnet		5.10 ¤ Stretch Cap, White		0.90 ¤ Pony-O's 6 Pack	2	0.75 ¤ Black Pony Tail Rubber bands	
5.50 ¤ Shaving Shower Bag, Clear		0.35 ¤ Clothes Hanger	5	1.95 ¤ Sewing Kit		1.40 ¤ Typewriter Correction Tape	
8.55 ¤ Typewriter Ribbon, Large		7.15 ¤ Typewriter Ribbon, Small		14.30 ¤ Dr. Scholl's Gel Shoe Insoles		2.35 ¤ Odor Absorbing Shoe Insoles	
		5.00 ¤ Kiwi Shoe Brush		1.15 ¤ Shoe Laces [Black]-[White]		1.55 ¤ White Envelope Box	
1.50 ¤ Transparent Envelope	5	0.15 ¤ Yellow Manila Envelope	5	1.10 ¤ White Writing Pad	2	1.45 ¤ Yellow Legal Pad	2
2.00 ¤ Pens 2 Pack [Black]-[Blue]	2	1.10 ¤ Pen Refills [Black]-[Blue]	2	2.60 ¤ Playing Cards	2	2.60 ¤ Pinochle Cards	2
9.65 ¤ Chess Set		12.00 ¤ Double Nine Dominos		4.50 ¤ Double Six Dominos		3.80 ¤ Replacement Bulbs 4.8 Volt	
1.30 ¤ Replacement Bulb 2.5 Volt		11.70 ¤ L.E.D. Book Light		1.80 ¤ Photo Album		3.15 ¤ Address Book	
17.65 ¤ Liquid Slip 2 Gallon Box							

Grooming Aids [Limit 1 Each]

5.15 ¤ Mustache Scissors	0.80 ¤ Finger nail Clippers	1.05 ¤ Toenail Clippers	1.05 ¤ Tweezers
4.05 ¤ Beard, Hair removal Cream	7.65 ¤ Magnum Razor Refills 4 Pack	2.35 ¤ Blue Shave Powder	3.65 ¤ Head, Hair Removing Cream
7.65 ¤ Magnum Razor	1.70 ¤ Shaving Gel	5.15 ¤ Mach 3 Razor	12.35 ¤ Mach 3 Razor Refills 3 Pack
2.25 ¤ Disposable Razors 5 Pack	4.00 ¤ Bump Stopper	5.95 ¤ Kiss My Face Shave Cream	1.10 ¤ Cotton Swabs
3.70 ¤ Gillette Aftershave			

Skin Care [Limit 1 Each]

6.00 ¤ Cocoa Butter Lotion	3.00 ¤ CK-1 Lotion	6.05 ¤ St. Ives Lotion	1.30 ¤ Aleeda Aloe Lotion
4.35 ¤ Quisana Foot Powder	3.00 ¤ Sun Block SPF 30	3.45 ¤ Neutrogena Facial Bar	1.35 ¤ Petroleum Jelly
2.20 ¤ Noxzema Cream	2.85 ¤ Coconut Oil	1.95 ¤ Cocoa Butter Stick	2.00 ¤ Blistex Lip Balm
3.05 ¤ Skin Tone Cream	2.20 ¤ Body Powder		

Hygiene [Limit 1 Each Unless Noted]

2.40 Speed Stick Fresh Deodorant	3.00 Ban Cool Sport Deodorant	3.50 Speed Stick Aqua Gel Deodorant	3.05 Secret Deodorant
2.45 Speed Stick Regular Deodorant	3.00 Sure Deodorant	5.00 Apricot Scrub	1.30 Antibacterial Liquid Soap
1.10 Tone Skin Care Soap 3	1.90 Ivory Soap 3 Pack	2.15 Irish Spring Soap 3 Pack	2.05 Dove Soap 3
0.85 Dial Soap	0.60 Soap Dish	1.20 Black Soap 3	

Dental [Limit 1 Each]

1.70 Denture Brush	5.30 Interdental Refills	2.05 Aim Mouth Wash	3.00 Colgate Whitening Toothpaste
2.85 Colgate Total Toothpaste	3.85 Colgate Max White Gel	2.70 Close Up Toothpaste	2.00 Aim Toothpaste
6.30 Sensodyne Toothpaste	4.65 Effergrip Dental Adhesive	1.45 Flosser / Gum Stimulator	1.70 Dental Floss
1.30 Denture Cup Bath	3.50 Denture Cleaner Paste	0.45 Toothbrush Holder	0.80 Toothbrush

Hair Care [Limit 1 Each Unless Noted]

2.25 Hair Spray	3.20 Styling Brush	0.85 Comb 7"	0.80 Afro Pick
0.75 Afro Comb	1.30 Club Brush	3.35 Styling Hair Gel	2.95 Protein 29 Hair Gel
	2.45 Murray's Pomade	5.40 Pink Moisturizer	3.20 Comb thru Softener
4.50 Softee 3n1 Shampoo	4.50 Softee 3n1 Conditioner	9.40 Relax System Conditioner Kit	2.40 Coconut Hair Conditioner
1.40 Dandruff Shampoo 2	7.30 Head & Shoulders Shampoo	2.75 Herbal Shampoo	6.10 Pantene Shampoo
5.95 Pantene Conditioner	2.15 Suave Shampoo	2.15 Suave Conditioner	3.90 Blue Magic Conditioner
5.75 Dr. Miracle Grow Balm	5.05 Dr. Miracle Braid Relief	7.15 Dr. Miracle 2 in 1 Shampoo	5.75 Dr. Miracle Treatment

Medical / Health Items [Limit 1 Unless Noted]

7.75 T / Gel Shampoo	2.25 Corn Cushions	6.85 Medicated Tucks Pads	7.50 Dibucaine Ointment 1 %
3.35 Band Aids			
2.35 Medicated Chest Rub	3.80 Hemorrhoid Ointment	1.65 Dr. Sheffield's Acne Cream	1.90 Calamine Lotion
1.45 Hydrocortisone Cream	1.90 Loperamide (Imodium) 2mg	2.40 Milk of Magnesia	3.70 Docusate
3.60 Vitamin A & D Ointment	2.50 Triple Antibiotic Ointment	14.30 Lac Hydrin 5 Lotion	1.60 Athlete Foot Cream Tolnaftate
8.30 Lamisil Generic	1.90 Antifungal Cream Clotrimazole	6.30 Orange Fiber Powder	1.80 Saline Nasal Spray
8.70 Breathe Right Strips [M] [L]	2.45 Loratadine, Claritin	1.60 Cold & Allergy Tabs	2.35 Cough Syrup
0.90 Honey / Lemon Cough Drops 2	0.90 Cherry Cough Drops 2	2.65 Cherry Lozenges	1.55 Muscle Balm
1.90 Ibuprofen 200 mg	4.95 Naproxen Pain Relief, Aleve	2.05 Acetaminophen Non-Aspirin	1.85 Low Dose Aspirin 81 mg
1.10 Aspirin 325 mg	1.30 Oral Pain Relief	1.90 Ear Drops	10.60 Allergy Eye Drops Opcon-A
2.85 Eye Drops Lubricant	2.10 Calcium 250 mg	3.65 Vitamin E 400 mg	1.95 Vitamin C 500 mg
2.50 Vitamin B Complex	4.60 Antacid Gaviscon	7.30 Lactaid [Dairy Supplement]	3.00 Multi Vitamin
3.20 Simethicone, Anti Gas	17.65 Prilosec	3.35 Antacid, Double Strength Liquid	2.15 Tums 3 Pack 2
3.75 Ranitidine (Zantac)			

Sundry Items [Limit 1 Each]

3.90 Fragrance Oil Specify	1.85 Trend Detergent [FPC ONLY]	6.60 Tide W/Bleach [FPC ONLY]	2.90 Bounce Dryer Sheets[FPC ONLY]
3.10 Charmin Toilet Paper	1.35 Ajax Dish Soap	6.75 Master Combination Lock	6.80 Solar Calculator
16.95 Scientific Calculator	19.10 Timex Watch	62.40 Casio G-Shock Watch	9.75 Velcro Watch Bands
3.90 Plastic Watch Band	11.45 Timex Watch Band	8.45 G-Shock Watch Band	8.80 Watch Band
8.80 Fits All Watch Band	2.60 Watch Battery #	28.95 Jenssen Digital Radio	42.00 Sony Digital Radio
0.65 Porta Pro Replacement Ear Pads	45.45 Koss Porta Pro Headphones	10.35 JVC Ear Buds	12.90 Sony Head Phones
1.50 Reading Glasses Specify	4.95 Microwave Bowl, Round W/Lid	1.05 Cutlery Set, 3pc	4.25 Insulated Mug, 64 oz
2.95 Squeeze Bottle	1.65 Coffee Mug 20 oz	9.35 Digital Alarm Clock	47.40 Sangean Radio
69.20 MP-3 Player	2.60 MP-3 Cover		

Clothing [Limit 1 Each] Specify Size If Necessary

6.00 Shower Shoes Generic Size 1	0.80 Handkerchief White	6.50 White Baseball Cap [S/M - L/XL] 3	7.80 Wigwam Sock 1pr [M-LG-XL]
5.20 Ankle Socks Med 3 Pack 1	1.45 Crew Sock 1pr	1.30 No Show Socks	1.45 Ankle Sock 1pr 3
5.85 XL Ankle Socks 3 pack 1	5.60 T-Shirt, Grey, Medium	5.60 T-Shirt, Grey, Large	5.60 T-Shirt, Grey, X-Large
5.60 T-Shirt, Grey, 2X-Large	5.60 T-Shirt; Grey, 3X-Large	5.60 T-Shirt, Grey, 4X-Large	11.70 T-Shirt, Grey, 5X-Large
16.90 D-Ups Shorts. [Sm-Med]	17.95 D-Ups Shorts [LG-XL-2X]	18.95 D-Ups Shorts [3X-4X]	14.00 D-Ups Shorts [6X-7X]
13.95 Sweat Shorts Medium	12.95 Sweat Shorts [LG-XL]	14.95 Sweat Shorts 2X-Large	14.95 Sweat Shorts 3X-Large
16.95 Sweat Shorts [4X-5X]	1.95 Washcloth, Beige	8.15 Beach Towel, Beige	2.65 Boxers, White Single (3) [S-M]
2.65 Boxers, White Single (3)[LG-XL]	3.50 Boxers, White Single 2X (3)	3.50 Boxers, White Single 3X (3)	7.15 Boxer Briefs Grey 2PK [M-LG]
7.15 Boxer Brief Grey 2PK [XL-2X]	7.80 Boxer Briefs Grey 2PK 3XL	7.80 Boxer Briefs Grey 2PK. 4XL	17.25 Sweat Shirt Large [M-L]
17.25 Sweat Shirt	19.95 Sweat Shirt 3X-Large	19.95 Sweat Shirt 4X-Large	24.95 Sweat Shirt 5X-Large
19.95 Sweat Pants [M, L, XL]	19.95 Sweat Pants 2X-Large	22.75 Sweat Shirt [3X-4X]	22.10 Sweat Pants 5X-Large
5.85 Thermal Shirt White [M]	6.25 Thermal Shirt White [L, XL]	7.80 Thermal Shirt White 2X-Large	9.90 Thermal Shirt White [3X]
10.75 Thermal Shirt White [4X]	14.55 Thermal Shirt White 5X-Large	10.40 Long Sleeve Shirt Grey [S-M]	10.40 Long Sleeve Shirt Grey [LG]
10.40 Long Sleeve Shirt Grey [XL]	10.40 Long Sleeve Shirt Grey [2X-3X]	10.40 Long Sleeve Shirt Grey [4X]	10.40 Long Sleeve Shirt Grey [5X]
	16.90 Reebok Sandal Size ___		
Recreational [Limit 1 Each]			
8.90 Weight Lifting Gloves [M-LG-XL-2X]	11.70 Eye Protection	5.20 Racquetballs 3Pack	14.30 Racquetball Glove[L-R][M-LG-XL]
5.20 Clip-On Sunglasses	15.35 Weight Lifting Gloves [LG-XL]	18.20 Waist Trimmer [S-M-LG-2X]	5.20 Sunglass Croakies
5.20 Jock Strap [M]	6.50 Sunglasses	1.75 Headband	1.70 Wristband
5.20 Jock Strap [LG-XL]	11.70 Knee Support [M-LG-XL]	3.00 Insect Repellant	9.10 Mesh Gym Bag
Religious Items [Limit 3 Each]			
5.25 ¤ Stuffed Cabbage Kosher Meal	5.25 ¤ Bone-N-Chicken Kosher Meal	4.15 Beef Goulash Kosher Meal	8.00 ¤ Beef Rib Steak Kosher Meal
19.00 Rasta Crown [L-XL]	6.82 * Yarmulkes, White	6.82 * Yarmulkes, Black	3.50 * Kufi
2.69 Bandana [Black-Red]	4.90 ¤ Chicken Matza Ball Soup	5.95 ¤ Gefilte Fish Kosher	
Greeting Cards [Limit 3 Each]			
1.40 Greeting Cards #[ ] #[ ] #[ ]			

Prices may vary due to changes by the vendor. You must turn in your own list and have proper identification to shop. If you are not in the commissary area when your name is called, you will lose your shopping privileges for the week. No changes or substitutions will be allowed at the window. Account balances will not be checked during, sales. The commissary staff may limit the quantities at their discretion. All sales are final. Items marked with "¤" have an acceptable Kosher and/or Halal sign. Items marked with "*" require authorization prior to the purchase. Stamps and medical / health products do not affect your monthly spending limit.

Approved by: Nanette Barnes, A.W.(O&P)   Approved by: Rob Wilson, Warden

Appendix B

Appendix B

Federal Correctional Institution
Federal Prison Camp
Miami, Florida

ADMISSION & ORIENTATION
HANDBOOK

English Edition

Revised March 2009

****
****

The information contained in this handbook is current, as of the publication. It contains summaries of Bureau of Prisons Program Statements and FCI & FPC Miami, Institution Supplements and is subject to change. It is intended to be used by staff and inmates of this facility as an easy reference, but policy always takes precedence over information contained within this document.

TABLE OF CONTENTS

WARDEN'S INTRODUCTION

The Federal Correctional Institution, Miami, Florida is located at 15801 SW 137th Avenue, and was dedicated on March 26, 1976, as a facility under the jurisdiction of the United States Department of Justice, Federal Bureau of Prisons.

Our mission is to provide a safe, humane, and secure facility. While here, you have certain rights and responsibilities, which are explained in this booklet. We expect you to behave appropriately, while following the rules and regulations. You are being provided with this handbook in order to give you a general overview of the Institution's rules, regulations, and programs. Additional information will be provided during the Admission and Orientation (A&O) process. You may also review Bureau of Prisons, Program Statements and FCI Miami, Institution Supplements, available in the law library.

This Institution offers a wide variety of educational and self improvement opportunities. Accordingly, what you gain during your stay here will depend largely on you. Sanitation and personal hygiene are very important in communal living. You are required to maintain a high level of personal cleanliness, and assist in the general cleaning of your housing unit. Staff will make every effort to meet your basic needs while you, on the other hand, will be expected to provide good work habits and a positive attitude. Violations of institution rules and/or regulations will not be tolerated.

Read this booklet carefully and keep it in your possession. If you have any questions, ask your unit team.

Kenny Atkinson
Warden

1

ADMISSION AND ORIENTATION (A&O)

Each inmate committed or transferred to a Bureau of Prisons institution is required to attend the Institution's A&O Program. This program is intended to familiarize you with the institution and give you an awareness of:

(1) Inmate's rights and responsibilities;
(2) Institution's program opportunities;
(3) Institution disciplinary system; and
(4) Institution operations

This program consists of presentations from designated representatives of each department within the institution. The program should provide answers to many of the questions you may have about our facility. The A&O program is conducted in the Chapel on alternate Wednesdays.

Until removed from A&O status, each inmate will be accountable to the Unit Officer. Unit Officers will ensure that the inmate:

1. Checks the "CALL-OUT" daily for Medical and Educational Screening appointments.
2. Assigned to work in the unit as needed.
3. Attends Institution A&O Presentation pursuant to call out.

Upon completion of the A&O Program, your medical screening should be completed and you will be assigned to a work detail.

Upon commitment, you were given a Federal Register Number that will be used to identify you while in federal custody. All mail and money orders must be identified with your (committed) name and register number to ensure it is promptly processed and received.

UNIT MANAGEMENT

Unit Management's mission is to determine inmate program needs, and monitor participation to encourage pro-social institution and community behaviors that benefit inmates, staff, victims and society. This is accomplished through functional unit management and effective interaction with inmates.

A Unit Manager, who supervises the other primary unit team members, including Case Managers, Correctional Counselors, and Unit Secretary, heads each team. The team also includes the unit officers, an Education Advisor, and Psychologist, each of whom fulfills a distinct and vital role.

The primary responsibility of the unit staff is to ensure that mandates of the court are implemented. Secondly, they are responsible for providing a safe and humane environment for inmates and staff. The unit team plans, develops, supervises and coordinates individual programs tailored to meet the particular needs of inmates in the unit. Unit staff are available each day of the week and most evenings until 9:00 P.M.

ROLES OF THE UNIT TEAM

Unit Manager:
Responsible for the unit's operation and security, within appropriate policy, as well as for planning, developing, implementing, supervising, and coordinating individual programs tailored to meet the particular needs of inmates in the unit.

Case Manager:
Responsible for all casework services and prepares classification material, progress reports, release plans, transfers, correspondence, and other documentation relating to your commitment. They serve as a liaison with the administration, Community Corrections Center personnel, and criminal justice authorities. The Case Manager provides necessary services to each
inmate to help him/her adjust to the institution environment and prepare for eventual release.

Under the provisions of Title 18, U.S. Code, Section 4004, your Case Manager is authorized to notarize documents. However, due to a recent change in the law, notarization is not required if you include a statement to the effect that the papers which you are signing are "true and correct under a penalty of perjury" some states will not accept a government notarization for real state transactions, automobile

3

sales, power of attorney, etc. In these cases, it will be necessary to arrange for a Florida Notary.

Correctional Counselor:

Provides counseling and guidance for you in areas of institution adjustment and plans for the future. They are responsible for establishing and maintaining visiting lists and phone list. The Counselor is the individual to approach with personal difficulties, such as administrative complaints, visiting, room changes, mail, property, and initial and/or change of work assignments. Counselors conduct individual and group counseling and assists inmates in resolving day to day problems.

Unit Secretary:

Assists the unit team by performing clerical and administrative functions. Including but not limited to the maintenance of inmate central files and paperwork necessary for an inmate release and Unit operations.

Correctional Officers:

Responsible for day-to-day accountability and supervision of inmates. They have direct responsibility for safety, security, and sanitation of the unit. Officers are on duty around the clock.

UNIT PROGRAM, SERVICES AND ACTIVITIES

Your Unit Team will assist you in planning and accomplishing your program goals in preparation for your release. **YOU** are the most important member of the team, and your accomplishments depend upon your own desires and

motivation. Informational bulletin boards are located in each housing unit. You are expected to review the information on these boards daily. Schedules of activities, changes in rules and regulations, call outs, and/or special events are posted on the bulletin boards.

Town Hall Meetings:

Are conducted monthly or as deemed necessary by the Unit Manager, attendance is mandatory. These meetings are held to make announcements and to discuss changes in policy and provide needed information. Inmates are encouraged to ask pertinent questions. These questions should pertain to the unit as a whole, rather than personal questions or problems. Personal problems will be resolved in private meetings with your unit staff.

Program Reviews:

The Unit Team will meet with you and formally review your program every 90 days, if you are within one year of your release date, and every 180 days for the remaining population. Attendance for your program review is mandatory. You should be prepared to discuss your Institutional progress and any request you have. Consideration for transfers, community corrections center placement, job changes, and similar modifications in your program will normally be handled during these team meeting.

Progress Reports:

When a progress report is prepared, you will be given the opportunity to review it, and you will receive a copy. You will be ask to sign the cover page indicating, you have received a copy. Your signature does not indicate your agreement with the contents of the report.

Central Inmate Monitoring System(CIMS):

Refers to the procedures by which the BOP monitors and controls the transfer and participation in community activities of inmates who pose special management consideration. The designation as a CIMS case does not, in and of itself, preclude an inmate from transfer consideration or participation in community activities. Your Case Manager will notify you if you are placed in (CIMS).

Savings Account:

To establish a savings account, you need to contact:

Community Bank of Alabama
P.O. Box 9
Union Town, Alabama 36786
Attn: Ms. Vanette B. Caine
Asst. Vice President

In the event you need assistance, your unit counselor will be able to assist you

Release Gratuities:

Are monies given upon release. This amount is based on individual need. The case Management Coordinator will be responsible for determining the financial needs of the inmate nearing release. Release transportation expenses will be provided to an inmate's release destination or halfway house location.

COMMISSARY

The Commissary is located next to Food Service and operates for the benefit of the inmates. Inmates who have funds posted in their commissary account will be permitted to spend up to $290.00 monthly for a variety of articles.
HOWEVER, EVERYTHING THAT YOU BUY MUST FIT NEATLY INSIDE YOUR LOCKER WITH YOUR CLOTHING AND PERSONAL ITEMS.

Stamps and over the counter (OTC) medical items are not discounted from the monthly spending limit.

ALL SALES ARE FINAL AFTER YOU HAVE SIGNED YOUR RECEIPT. NO CHANGES OR RETURNS ARE ALLOWED UNDER ANY CIRCUMSTANCES.

Commissary hours are posted in the housing areas, as well as at the bulletin board in front of the commissary. The commissary schedule is based on the fourth and fifth digit of your Inmate Register Number. For example, if your number is: 12389-004, 89 is the number which will identify your date of purchase.

First time shoppers can shop any day of the week by identifying their list as "First Time Shopper."

The shopping schedule is rotated on a quarterly basis as follows:

	Tuesday	Wednesday	Thursday	Friday
January-March	00-24	25-49	50-74	75-99
April-June	75-99	00-24	25-49	50-74
July-September	50-74	75-99	00-24	25-49
October-December	24-49	50-74	75-99	00-24

2:00 P.M. - 3:00 P.M.	Conduct sales to unit orderlies, Recreation A.M. Workers and Food Service A.M. workers.
3:00 P.M. - 3:30 P.M.	Conduct sales to UNICOR overtime workers when needed.
After 4:00 P.M. Count	Sales will resume for the remainder of the compound. Last call will be at 5:30 P.M., if needed.

Validation is the renewal of your spending limit each month. The validation schedule is based on the fifth digit of your Inmate Register Number as indicated on the shopping schedule. Validation date is determined by multiplying the 5th digit of the register # by 3 and then adding 1 (If the 5th digit is 3, the validation date would be the 10th, for example: $3 * 3 = 9 + 1 = 10$).

Each inmate must have an identification card to shop. Inmates must carry the I.D. card at all times. Vending credits may be purchased and stored on the identification cards. This makes the card the same as money and should be safeguarded as such.

All Special Housing Unit orders will be delivered to the unit by commissary staff before the 4:00 P.M. count on Friday. If the delivery is not possible, the commissary officer will attempt to deliver on another day. If delivery cannot be completed on either day, the order will be canceled and the inmate account credited.

The purchase receipt must be signed by the inmate prior to taking possession of the items. All sales are final.

No claims will be honored unless it is brought to the attention of the Commissary Clerk at the time of sale.

Checking account balance and notes:

Inmates may check their account balance using the Automated Inquiry Machine (AIM) located at the commissary window by utilizing their PIN number (Type: Register number, PIN number). PIN numbers can be obtained in the Business Office, Inmate's Account Section, on Tuesdays and Thursdays from 11:00 A.M. to noon. Account balances can also be obtained via the ITS-II system (instructions are provided in that section).

Any inmate who is not in line 15 minutes before closing will not be served and any inmate who does not respond when his name is called will lose the shopping privilege for the week. The commissary will be closed the last week of each quarter for inventory.

7

COMMUNITY CORRECTIONS CENTER PLACEMENT

Inmates nearing release, who need assistance in obtaining a job, residence or other community resources, may be transferred to a Community Corrections Center(CCC).

CCC's provide a suitable residence, job placement, and counseling while monitoring the offender's activities.

They also provide drug/alcohol testing, counseling, and treatment. While in the program, employed offenders are required to pay subsistence to help defray the cost of their confinement. The payment rate is 25% of the inmate's income.

Each CCC now provides two components within one facility a pre-release component and a community corrections component. The pre-release component assists offenders making the transition from an Institution setting to the community, or as a resource while under supervision.

The community corrections component is designed as a punitive sanction. Except for employment and other required activities, the offenders in this second, more restrictive component, must remain at the CCC where recreation, visiting and other activities are provided in-house.

CULTURAL DIVERSITY

The correctional environment is a multi-cultural environment that may cause some to experience discomfort. Your attitude about diversity, along with respect for others is important if you want to live harmoniously in this setting.

Respect begins with the self and extends to others in our actions, and/or behaviors. You will be exposed to different races, classes, ages, cultures, and religions. While our personal experiences, beliefs, training, education, religion and value systems affect our attitudes through cross-cultural experiences we can became more tolerant.

The Bureau of Prisons has a ZERO TOLERANCE policy on any form or level of discrimination and/or violence. Psychology Services offers programs to minimize the negative impact of intolerance.

EDUCATION DEPARTMENT

FCI Miami Education Department offers a variety of programs to meet the varied needs of the inmate population. All inmates are interviewed to determine their educational and testing needs as part of the A&O process.

Effective May 1, 1991, the Federal Bureau of Prisons increased the literacy requirement to a High School Diploma or equivalence. All inmates who do not have a verified High School Diploma or equivalence are required to attend a GED Preparation class for a period of 240 instructional hours or until successful passing of the GED Exam. You will be given the (TABE) TEST OF ADULT BASIC EDUCATION, interviewed by an Education staff member, and placed in the appropriate class if needed. An inmate will not receive approval to voluntarily withdraw from the literacy program until he completes at least 240 instructional hours in the program. Inmates under **VCCLEA**[1] and **PLRA**[2] could have their Good Conduct Time affected if not enrolled and actively participating in the GED program. An incentive award of Five (5) dollars is given to an inmate who completes the TABE program, while Twenty-Five (25) dollars is awarded to those who pass the GED or ESL examinations.

Other classes offered by the Education Department are: (ESL) English as a Second Language, Parenting, Janitorial, Pre-Release Preparation, College and other Correspondence Courses, Drafting VT, Computer-Aided Business Education VT, Apprenticeship programs such as Plumbing, Electrician, Heating and Air Conditioning, Landscape Technician. In the evening, (ACE) Adult Continuing Education courses and some GED remedial classes are available.

The Law, Leisure and Media Lab Libraries are located in the Education Building. They are equipped with books, forms, newspapers, magazine, and typewriters. Audio-visual equipment such as cassette players and TV/VCRS are available for check out to be used within the department. There is also an Interlibrary Loan whereby inmates can borrow up to five books form the Florida Interlibrary Loan Department. All Interlibrary Loan books must be returned by the due date, otherwise charges are assessed. The library hours are Mon-Thur 7:30 A.M.-8:00 P.M., Fri 7:30 A.M.-3:00 P.M. and Sat 7:30 A.M.-3:30 P.M. There is also an "out-

---

[1] The **VCCLEA** (Violent Crime Control Act) mandates that an inmate whose offense was on or after September 13, 1994, but before April 26, 1996, and who lacks a high school credential, participates in and makes satisfactory progress toward attaining a General Education Development (GED) credential in order to vest earned Good Conduct Time (GCT).

[2] The **PLRA** (Prison Litigation Reform Act) provides that, in determining GCT awards, the Bureau will consider whether an inmate, with a date of offense on or after April 26, 1996, who lacks a high school credential, participates and makes satisfactory progress toward attaining a GED credential, in order to be eligible to earn the maximum amount of GCT.

count" available on <u>Saturdays</u> to permit inmates to remain in the Law/Leisure Library during the 10:00 A.M. count. Those wishing to sign up for the out-count must sign up in the "out-count book" located in the Law Library by noon on the Friday before and must be present in Library by 9:00 A.M. on Saturday.

This institution has implemented an Electronic Law Library System (ELL). The ELL is a useful tool enabling you to conduct any legal research you may have. Inmate Law Clerks are available during all ELL hours to assist you with accessing the ELL, as well as to teach you how to use all features of this program.

If you are interested in any of the aforementioned programs, please present a cop-out or inmate request to the Education Department for enrollment or stop by to obtain more information.

FACILITIES

The Facilities Department at FCI Miami is responsible for the management of all construction, repairs, improvements and maintenance to the physical plant. Also included under this operation is all equipment and utilities of all major operating units, along with energy conservation.

The facilities operation offers a variety of work relating to construction and maintenance trades.

Typical trades within this departments are: auto repairs, electronics, carpentry, electric, masonry, paint, plumbing, landscape and general maintenance shops. This operation employs approximately 203 inmates within the FCI and 91 inmates at the Federal Prison Camp.

All inmates interested in obtaining a work assignment in this department may submit an "Inmate Request to Staff Member: (COP-OUT) to the Facilities Manager. Starting pay is generally from $.12 an hour for grade 4 on a 7 hour work day and may progress up to grade 1 which is $.40 per hour. Promotions are based on job knowledge, performance, general attitude, cooperation with staff and fellow inmates and compliance with safety and sanitation policies and regulations.

FINANCIAL MANAGEMENT

Inmate funds are retained by the institution in a Deposit Fund account, established in your name, in the Office of Financial Management, which reflects all of your deposits and withdrawals.

You may withdraw money for personal spending in the Commissary, family support, or other approved purposes. Institutional earnings and money sent from the outside are given to you upon release, or may be mailed home.

The Federal Bureau of Prisons requires that all funds being mailed to inmates be sent to the Federal Bureau of Prisons' national Lockbox. If you wish to have funds sent to you, while incarcerated in the Federal Bureau of Prisons, please have them sent to the following address:

Federal Bureau of Prisons
***Insert* Inmate Name**
***Insert* Inmate Register Number**
Post Office Box 474701
Des Moines, Iowa 50947-0001

In order to ensure that your funds are processed without delay to the inmate's Trust Fund account, you must adhere to the following directions:

The inmate's committed name (no nicknames) and register number must be printed on all envelopes and enclosed allowable instruments (U.S. Postal and Western Union money orders; U.S. Treasury, State, and Local Government checks; any foreign negotiable instruments payable in U.S. currency).

Senders must enclose only the allowable negotiable instrument. DO NOT enclose cash, personal checks, letters, pictures or any other items in the envelope. The national Lockbox cannot forward any items enclosed with the allowable negotiable instrument to the inmate. Items, personal in nature, must be mailed directly to the Federal Bureau of Prisons' institution where the inmate is housed. The senders name and return address must appear on the upper left hand corner of the envelope to ensure that their funds can be returned to them in the event that they cannot be posted to the inmate's account

All domestic checks will be held for at least fifteen (15) days before being posted to the inmates's account. All foreign checks will be held for sixty (60) days before being posted. Money earned will be credited to your commissary account when payroll is posted.

11

Funds can now be sent via Western Union's Quick Collect Program by going to an agent location with cash, by phone using a credit/debit card, or online using a credit/debit card. For each Western Union Quick Collect transaction, the following information must be provided:

Inmate Register Number
Inmate Name
City Code: FBOP
State Code: DC

Western Union will charge the public as little as $3.95 for US Cash transfers up to $5,000 processed at Western Union agent locations. Transfers via the telephone or Internet have higher fees. Non-US transfers also have higher fees.

All funds sent via Western Union's Quick Collect will be posted to the inmate's account within Two (2) to Four (4) hours, when those funds are sent between 7:00 a.m. and 9:00 p.m. EST. Funds received after 9:00 p.m. EST will be posted by 9:00 a.m. EST the following morning.

Request for Withdrawal of Personal Funds (BP-199.045) shall be prepared using the TRULINCS computer system. After entering necessary information, users must go to Education to print the form and turn it in to a member of appropriate Unit Team. This form is utilized when you wish to purchase a subscription, send funds home, deposit funds in a savings account, etc.

Money is distributed by a U.S. Treasury check from the Regional Disbursing Office, Treasury Department. It takes approximately Twenty (20) days to reach its point of delivery. The Associate Warden must approve any withdrawals exceeding $ 250.00.

Upon commitment, you will be given an I.D. card with your register number and picture. This card is required for your commissary purchases and for positive visual identification by staff. Your card must be in your possession at all times. You will be charged a $5.00 replacement fee should you lose or destroy your card. If you change your appearance, (beard/hair shaved) you are required to purchase a replacement card at your expense.

The Commissary offers a variety of products. The purpose is to provide inmates with merchandise not provided by the Bureau of Prisons and food items to complement the Institution Food Service menu. Commissary use is a privilege, not a right.

Empty containers must be discarded and not used for any other purpose.

Shopping in the commissary is limited to once per week except for over the counter (OTC) medical items. The commissary price/order list forms are given out at the Commissary for the next weeks purchases. Out-of-stocks items, new items and price changes are posted at the commissary. Substitution are limited to out-of-stock or new items with like items only.

FINANCIAL RESPONSIBILITY PROGRAM (FRP)

The Bureau of Prisons strongly encourages you to satisfy your legitimate financial obligations (e.g., special assessments, committed fines, non-committed fines, court ordered restitution, fines and court cost, child support, alimony, etc.).

As part of the initial classification process, your Unit Team will provide you with the opportunity to develop a financial plan for satisfying these obligations. You are responsible for making all payments required, either from earnings within the Institution or from outside resources. You must provide documentation of compliance and payment.

Although this is a voluntary program, if you refuse to meet your obligations, you can neither work for **UNICOR** nor receive performance pay above the maintenance pay level ($5.25 per month). Institution assignments such as the Yard, Recreation, Trash Detail, Orderly or visiting Room needs the Associate Warden of Programs approval if you are in refusal status. You will also be held to a $25.00 per month spending limit for commissary excluding purchase of stamps, telephone credits and allowable common fare participant entrees. You will not be allowed to participate in the Pre-Release Halfway House Program.

If you have a substantial fine, you may, at the recommendation of the Unit Team, be placed on the UNICOR priority hiring list. Such placement would allow for accelerated payment of monies due.

During subsequent program reviews, your Team will consider your willingness and dedication to addressing your legal Financial Responsibility Program (FRP), this factor will be assessed when considering you for various programs.

The U.S. Parole Commission will also review financial responsibility progress at parole hearings. The lack of institution earnings does not exclude you from developing a financial plan.

NOTE:

Unless otherwise ordered by a court, interest will accrue on the unpaid balance of your fine during your period of incarceration.

For detailed information concerning this program, contact your Unit Team or review the Program Statement in the Law Library.

FOOD SERVICE

The Food Service Department provides meals which are nutritionally adequate, properly prepared, and attractively served. All meals are served cafeteria style which includes features such as a salad bar, heat healthy options and flesh alternative programs. Special diets for religious and/or medical purposes must be approved through the Chaplain or medical staff.

General practices regarding the serving and portioning of menu food items require that meats, desserts, fresh fruits, and assorted dry cereals be rationed. One portion per individual. All other menu items are open.

After you finish eating, remember to leave your area as clean as possible. There is another individual waiting to sit at your table. Take your tray and all utensils to the dish room window. No food service utensils or food items.

Meal Hours:

Monday - Friday:	Breakfast	6:00 A.M. - 7:00 A.M.
	Lunch	10:45 A.M. - 12 Noon
	Dinner	After 4:00 P.M. - Count
Weekends/Holidays:	Breakfast	7:00 A.M. - 7:30 A.M.
	Brunch	After 10:00 A.M. - Count
	Dinner	After 4:00 P.M. - Count

NOTE:

A lieutenant is in charge of releasing inmates for meals. A set schedule is maintained by the Lieutenant's office using the results of the weekly sanitation inspection. The Inspection Team is appointed by the Warden or other personnel designated. The results of this inspection establishes the feeding order for specific housing units being called to mainline on a weekly basis.

All areas of the housing unit is inspected and scored with a numerical rating from 50 to 00. The unit with the highest rating will be called first, the second highest score called next and so on. A score of 25 or below loses T.V. privileges!

The following rules must be adhered to while you are in the dining area:

1.   Do not cut in line.

2.   Whistling, and boisterous conduct is not permitted.

3.   No personal cup/beverage containers, radios, books, bag, or laundry items are allowed in the dining room.

All inmates assigned to a Food Service Detail must maintain a high level of personal hygiene and wear appropriate clothing. Inmates must also receive medical clearance prior to F/S assignment.

All inmates assigned to the department have the opportunity to acquire skills and abilities that may assist them in obtaining gainful employment after release.

The Food Service Staff are always available to hear your comments and suggestions.

GROOMING

Appearance is important in making a positive impression on others, as well as providing you with a feeling of general well being and personal satisfaction. You are expected to maintain a neat and clean personal appearance at all times. It is your responsibility to keep yourself clean and well groomed.

Institution clothing will be worn during the normal workday, except for those inmates going to the recreation yard. The hours of the work day is from 7:30 a.m to 4:00 p.m. You will have your shirts neatly tucked in and pants will be fitted with a belt. Pants will be worn appropriately around the waist. The pant leg will

15

not be bloused, flared, or altered from issued condition. The T-shirt must be tucked in. If you desire to wear a sweat shirt, the sweat shirt must be tucked in. Safety shoes are required in work areas.

All FCI inmates will wear a black belt with the exception of the inmates in the ICAN program, who will wear a white belt. Relaxed dress will be allowed in the dining room during the evening and weekend meals. Relaxed dress includes shorts or sweat pants with T-shirt or sweat shirts, shoes and socks must be worn.

Head gear, other than religious, is restricted to baseball style caps, without insignia, emblems, or decorations, and will be worn facing forward at all times.

There is no restriction on hair style or length of hair; however, hair will be clean and neatly groomed at all times. If it is likely that long hair will result in a work injury, hair nets or caps will be worn. Beard masks will be required for persons working around food.

Camp dress code exception is green pants and shirts.

BARBER SERVICES

Hair care services are available to all inmates including Special Housing Unit. The Barber Shop is located in the Recreation building. The hours of operation are Monday through Thurday, from 12:30 P.M. to 3:00 P.M., and 5:30 P.M. to 8:00 P.M. The Barber Shop will be closed on Holidays. Any non-barber caught using barber tools will face disciplinary action.

Camp barber hours are Friday, Saturday and Monday, from 12:30 P.M. to 3:00 P.M., and 5:30 P.M. to 8:00 P.M. Camp barbershop is located in the multipurpose building, across from the commissary area.

HEALTH SERVICES

The Health Services Unit at FCI Miami provides medical coverage to all inmates from 6 A.M. to 10 P.M. The staff consists of a Clinical Director, physicians, dentist, physician assistants, registered nurses, x-ray technician, health information technicians, two assistant health services administrators, pharmacist and Health Services Administrator.

The consultant staff consists of various specialty physicians, a dental assistant, dental hygienist, and allied health technician pharmacist. Local emergency services include various community hospitals and the county fire/rescue squad.

PHYSICAL EXAMINATIONS:

Upon arrival at this facility all new inmates, requiring a physical examination, will be scheduled for admission blood work, x-rays, and a physical examination by placing your name in the "CALL-OUT." This is mandatory for all inmates. Medical duty status will be determined at this time and forwarded to the Unit Team.

A&O's and physical exams are normally conducted on Thursdays. It is your responsibility to watch for your name on the call-out sheet for scheduled appointments in the hospital.

Inmates under 50 years of age shall be offered a complete physical exam every two years. Inmates aged 50 and over are eligible for a complete physical examination annually to include EKG, Tonometry and digital rectal examination.

An inmate being release from the system may request a medical evaluation if he has not had one within 1 year prior to the expected date of release . Such examination should be conducted within two month prior to release. You must request this physical exam via cop-out to medical records.

Inmates are responsible for being present at their scheduled appointments. Violators will be subject to disciplinary action.

HIV (AIDS), TUBERCULOSIS, AND HEPATITIS:

An **HIV** detection program is in place at this facility. Any inmate requesting voluntarily the **HIV** test will be given one. This petition has to be requested through a **COP-OUT** to the Infectious Disease Coordinator. During the year, several **RANDOM TESTING**, will take place among the population and inmates will be selected through a computerized census drawing.

All inmates clinically suspected of having **HIV** will be tested. All inmates designated at this facility will be required to take an **HIV** examination before their release. The results of all test will be treated confidentially and counseling sessions will be available.

All inmates arriving at this facility will receive a **PPD** test. This test is designed to detect exposure to Tuberculosis. A positive test result reveals that the individual was exposed to the disease but does **NOT** indicate that the person has an active form and presents any risk to others. All inmates that have a positive reaction will be given a Chest X-Ray and will be offered the proper treatment. Make sure the PPD test is read within 36 hours of your arrival by reporting it to the P.A. administering **"SICK CALL."** Inmates designated at FCI/FPC Miami will require a yearly PPD test if the previous test had been negative.

JOB SAFETY:

Job Safety is everyone's priority. Familiarize yourself with the safety rules established at your work site. Inmates are required, and instructed how, to use proper eye and ear protection. All injuries must be reported to the Health Services Unit within 24 hours of the incident.

SICK CALL

All inmates will be allowed to attend sick call. Appointments times are determined by the medical staff.

Except for emergencies, sick call will be by appointment only, Mondays, Tuesdays, Wednesdays and Fridays excluding holidays.

Appointments will made from 6:30 to 7:00 A.M. at the FCI Hospital Annex building (behind the Lieutenant's office), inmates will be given a specific time to be seen by a health care provider.

Those appointments will begin at 8:00 A.M. and extend until 3:00 P.M. with a break for lunch from 11:00 A.M. to 12:00 noon. You are expected to be on time for your appointment.

Inmates are responsible for making and keeping their sick call appointments. Give the appointment slip to the detail officer upon reporting to work. The detail officer is responsible for releasing the inmates in time to make it to the hospital at the designated time. Inmates reporting late for appointments will be required to obtain a sick call appointment the following day unless their medical status dictates immediate treatment. All inmates reporting to sick call at the time of the appointment will be seen by a physician assistant (PA). Individuals who specifically request to see a doctor will be scheduled at the first available appointment.

18

SPECIAL HOUSING UNIT(SHU):

All **SHU** inmates will have the opportunity to see a physician assistant every day of the week. Sick Call rounds will be conducted everyday starting at 5:30 A.M. by the physician's assistants. Emergencies will be evaluated and treated as necessary.

EMERGENCY TREATMENT:

All inmates requiring emergency medical treatment, as determined by the medical staff, will be evaluated as soon as possible. If you are injured or require immediate medical care, you should inform your detail officer without delay, who will in turn contact the hospital. Routine complaints of non-emergency nature will not be treated as an emergency basis.

INPATIENT TREATMENT:

The need for outside hospitalization in a community hospital will be determined by the institution medical staff. In the event of life-threatening emergencies, fire/rescue and community hospital emergency rooms will be utilized.

MEDICATION:

All medications are issued by prescription only. When you are issued medication in a labeled container, it is for your use only and you should follow the directions exactly as written.

Controlled medication is issued on a per dose basis at the pill line window (Three times a day: 7:15 A.M. through 7:30 A.M.; 3:10 P.M. through 3:40 P.M. and 7:45 P.M. through 8:30 P.M.). On weekend and holidays, the morning pill line is from 8:00 A.M. through 8:15 A.M.

DENTAL AND EYE CARE:

Any inmate requiring emergency treatment due to severe tooth pain is eligible for dental sick call. Appointments will be obtained by inmates according to procedures outlined in the sick call section. Special Housing Unit inmates who require emergency dental treatment should inform the P.A. conducting sick call rounds.

All inmates with the necessity for eye care are required to attend "**Sick Call**." The individual will ask to be registered to see the Optometrist. An Optometrist is under contract and visits this facility on a as needed basis. Following a brief eye evaluation the inmate will be placed on a waiting list for the next available appointment.

Check the "Call Out" every day for your appointment.

NOTICE TO INMATES
INMATE CO-PAYMENT PROGRAM

Pursuant to the Federal Prisoner Health Care Co-payment Act (FHCCA) of 2000 (P.L. 106-294, 18 U.S.C. § 4048), The Federal Bureau of Prisons and FCI MIAMI, FLORIDA provide notice of the Inmate Co-payment Program for health care, effective October 3, 2005.

A. **Application:**

The Inmate Co-payment Program applies to anyone in an institution under the Bureau's jurisdiction and anyone who has been charged with or convicted of an offense against the United States, except inmates in inpatient status at a Medical Referral Center (MRC). All inmates in outpatient status at the MRCs and inmates assigned to the General Population at these facilities are subject to copy fees.

B. **Health Care Visits with a Fee:**

1. You must pay a fee of $2.00 for health care services, charged to your Inmate Commissary Account, per health care visit, if you receive health care services in connection with a health care visit that you requested, except for services described in section C., below.

   These requested appointments include Sick Call and after-hours requests to see a health care provider. If you ask a non-medical staff member to contact medical staff to request a medical evaluation on your behalf for a health service not listed in section C., below, you will be charged a $2.00 copy fee for that visit.

2. You must pay a fee of $2.00 for health care services, charged to your Inmate Commissary Account, per health care visit, if you are found responsible through the Disciplinary Hearing Process to have injured an inmate who, as a result of the injury, requires a health care visit.

C. **Health Care Visits with no Fee:**

We will not charge a fee for:

1. Health care services based on health care staff referrals;
2. Health care staff-approved follow-up treatment for a chronic condition;
3. Preventive health care services;
4. Emergency services;
5. Prenatal care;

20

6. Diagnosis or treatment of chronic infectious diseases;
7. Mental health care; or
8. Substance abuse treatment.

If a health care provider orders or approves any of the following, we will also not charge a fee for:

- Blood pressure monitoring;
- Glucose monitoring;
- Insulin injections;
- Chronic care clinics;
- TB testing;
- Vaccinations;
- Wound Care; or
- Patient education.

Your health care provider will determine if the type of appointment scheduled is subject to a copy fee.

D. **Indigence:**

An **indigent inmate** is an inmate who has not had a trust fund account balance of $6.00 for the past 30 days.

If you are considered indigent, you will not have the copy fee deducted from your Inmate Commissary Account.

If you are NOT indigent, but you do not have sufficient funds to make the copy fee on the date of the appointment, a debt will be established by TRUFACS, and the amount will be deducted as funds are deposited into your Inmate Commissary Account.

E. **Complaints:**

You may seek review of issues related to health service fees through the Bureau's Administrative Remedy Program (see 28 CFR part 542).

HEALTH CARE RIGHTS AND RESPONSIBILITIES

While in the custody of the Federal Bureau of Prisons you have the right to receive health care in a manner that recognizes your basic human rights, and you also accept the responsibility to cooperate with your health care plans and respect the basic human rights of your health care providers.

1. **Right:**
   You have the **right to access** health care services based on the local procedures at your institution. Health services include medical, dental and all support services. If inmate co-pay system exists in your institution, Health Services cannot be denied due to lack (verified)of personal funds to pay for your care.

   Responsibility:
   You have the responsibility to comply with the health care policies of your institution, and follow recommended treatment plans established for you, by health care providers. You have the responsibility to pay an identified fee for any health care encounter initiated by yourself, excluding emergency care. You will also pay the fee for the care of any other inmate on whom you intentionally inflict bodily harm or injury.

2. **Right:**
   You have the right to know the name and professional status of your health care providers and to be treated with respect, consideration and dignity.

   Responsibility:
   You have the responsibility to treat these providers as professionals and follow their instructions to maintain and improve your overall health.

3. **Right:**
   You have the right to address any concern regarding your health care to any member of the institution staff including the physician, the Health Services Administrator, members of your Unit Team, the Associate Warden and the Warden.

   Responsibility:
   You have the responsibility to address your concerns in the accepted format, such as the Inmate Request to Staff Member form, main line, or the accepted Inmate Grievance Procedures.

4. **Right:**
   You have the right to provide the Bureau of Prisons with Advance Directives or a Living Will that would provide the Bureau of Prisons with instructions if you are admitted as an inpatient to a hospital.

   Responsibility:
   You have the responsibility to provide the Bureau of Prisons with accurate information to complete this agreement.

5. **Right:**
    You have the right to be provided with information regarding your diagnosis, treatment and prognosis. This includes the right to be informed of health care outcomes that differ significantly from the anticipated outcome.
    Responsibility:
    You have the responsibility to keep this information confidential.

6. **Right:**
    You have the right to obtain copies of certain releasable portions of your health record.
    Responsibility:
    You have the responsibility to be familiar with the current policy and abide by such to obtain these records.

7. **Right:**
    You have the right to be examined in privacy.
    Responsibility:
    You have the responsibility to comply with security procedures should security be required during your examination.

8. **Right:**
    You have the right to participate in health promotion and disease prevention programs, including those providing education regarding infectious diseases.
    Responsibility:
    You have the responsibility to maintain your health and not to endanger yourself, or others, by participating in activity that could result in the spreading or catching an infectious disease.

9. **Right:**
    You have the right to report complaints of pain to your health care provider, have your pain assessed and managed in a timely and medically acceptable manner, be provided information about pain and pain management, as well as information on the limitations and side effects of pain treatments.
Responsibility:
    You have the responsibility to communicate with your health care provider honestly regarding your pain and your concerns about your pain.
    You also have the responsibility to adhere to the prescribed treatment plan and medical restrictions. It is your responsibility to keep your provider

informed of both positive and negative changes in your condition to assure timely follow up.

10. **Right:**

You have the right to receive prescribed medications and treatments in a timely manner, consistent with the recommendations of the prescribing health care provider.

Responsibility:

You have the responsibility to be honest with your health care provider(s), to comply with prescribed treatments and follow prescription orders. You also have the responsibility not to provide any other person your medication or other prescribed item.

11. **Right:**

You have the right to be provided healthy and nutritious food. You have the right to instruction regarding a healthy diet.

Responsibility:

You have the responsibility to eat healthy and not abuse or waste food or drink.

12. **Right:**

You have the right to request a routine physical examination, as defined by Bureau of Prisons' Policy. (If you are under the age of 50, once every two years; if over the age of 50, once a year and within one year of your release).

Responsibility:

You have the responsibility to notify medical staff that you wish to have an examination.

13. **Right:**

You have the right to dental care as defined in Bureau of Prisons' Policy to include preventative services, emergency care and routine care.

Responsibility:

You have the responsibility to maintain your oral hygiene and health.

14. **Right:**

You have the right to a safe, clean and healthy environment, including smoke-free living areas.

Responsibility:

You have the responsibility to maintain the cleanliness of personal and common areas and safety in consideration of others. You have the responsibility to follow the NO smoking regulations. It is occasionally necessary to restrict an inmate's activities for health reasons, without hospitalizing the inmate. The following are explanations of these types of restrictions.

Idle - An inmate must remain in his quarters except for meals, pill-line, sick-call, religious services, or Health Services Call-outs. The inmate is prohibited from participating in any work assignment or recreational activities. Idle slips should be displayed on the bunk or locker in full view for staff.

Convalescence - An inmate will not participate in any work assignment, but, he is not restricted to his quarters. He may not participate in strenuous recreational activity. He may engage in activities such as chess, checkers, and cards. If the inmate is enrolled in an education program, he must attend class unless specifically excused by written statement on the Convalescent form.

Medical Restriction - If medically indicated, an inmate will be placed on limited duty. Limited duty is prescribed when an inmate does not require an idle or convalescence but, does have medical restrictions which must be monitored on a work assignment.

Examples:
No lifting over (indicated) pounds, no prolonged walking or standing. Work restrictions will be specified on the Medical Duty Status Form.

INMATE DISCIPLINE

Inmates must have respect for the rights and property of others. You are urged to develop and exercise self-discipline. Rules, regulations, and policies are made to maintain a healthy and peaceful climate and to ensure an orderly operation of the facility. The inmate discipline policy has been developed to deal with those individuals who can not or will not exercise self-discipline.

Violation of regulations may result in an incident report and imposition of sanctions, as outlined later in this manual. In the event misconduct is observed by staff or there is evidence that misconduct has occurred, an incident report may be written by staff. This is the first step in the disciplinary process.
Incident reports are first investigated by a Lieutenant and the results forwarded to your Unit Team. The team meets as the Unit Discipline Committee (UDC) and may impose limited sanctions for most misconduct (for example, suspension of privileges, quarters change, job change, assigning extra duty, etc.).

If charges are more serious, the case will be referred to the Discipline Hearing Officer (DHO) who can impose more serious sanctions (for example forfeiture of good time, recommendation of transfer to a higher security level institution, or referral of the case to the F.B.I. for criminal action in a U.S. District Court). The internal disciplinary system is outlined in detail in Program Statement # 5270.07, which is available in the Law Library.

FCI Miami in accordance with BOP policy, will be a tobacco-free facility. Effective February 1, 2006, any inmate found to be in possession of any type of tobacco will be charged with possession of Anything Not Authorized, Code 305, and subject to disciplinary action.

Tables 1 and 2 provide a summary of the discipline system, while Table 3 provides a listing of prohibited acts by level of severity and shows the range of sanctions which may be imposed f+or violation of the institutional rules.

SUMMARY OF DISCIPLINARY SYSTEM
TABLE 1

PROCEDURE	DISPOSITION
1. Incident involving possible commission of a prohibited act.	1. Except for prohibited acts in the greatest or high severity categories, the writer of the report may resolve informally or drop the charges.
2. Staff prepares Incident Report and forwards it to the Lieutenant.	2. Except for prohibited acts in the greatest or high severity categories, the lieutenant may resolve informally or drop the charges.
3. An investigator will be appointed.	3. The investigator will conduct an investigation and forward the results to the UDC.
4. Initial hearing before the UDC.	4. The UDC may drop or resolve informally, any high, moderate, or low moderate charge, or impose allowable sanctions, or refer to DHO.
5. Hearing before (DHO).	5. The DHO may impose allowable sanctions or drop the charges.
6. Appeals through the Administrative Remedy procedure.	6. The Warden, Regional Director, or General Counsel may approve, modify, reverse, or remand with directions, including ordering a rehearing but, may not increase sanctions imposed.

TIME LIMITS IN DISCIPLINARY PROCESS
TABLE 2

7.   Staff becomes aware of inmate's involvement in incident.

   A.   **Ordinarily** maximum of 24 hours.

8.   Staff gives inmate notice of charges by delivering Incident Report.

   A.   Maximum ordinarily of 3 work days from the Time staff became aware of the inmate's involvement in the incident. (Excludes the day staff become aware of the inmate's involvement, weekends, and holidays).

9.   Initial Hearing (UDC).

   A.   Minimum of 24 hours. (Unless waived).

10.   Discipline Hearing Officer (DHO) Hearing.

NOTE:
These time limits are subject to exceptions as provided in the rules.

Staff may suspend disciplinary proceeding for a period not to exceed two calendar weeks while informal resolution is undertaken and accomplished. If informal resolution is unsuccessful, staff may re-institute disciplinary proceedings at the same stage at which suspended. The requirements then begin running again, at the same point at which they were suspended.

PROHIBITED ACTS AND
DISCIPLINARY SEVERITY SCALE
TABLE 3
GREATEST CATEGORY

NOTE:
The UDC shall refer all Greatest Severity prohibited acts to the DHO with recommendations as to an appropriate disposition.

CODE PROHIBITED ACTS	SANCTIONS
100 - Killing.	A. Recommend parole date rescission or retardation.
101 - Assaulting any person (includes sexual assault) or an armed assault on the institution's secure perimeter (a charge for assaulting any person at this level is to be used only when serious physical injury has been attempted or carried out by an inmate).	B. Forfeit earned statutory good time or non-vested good conduct time (up to 100%) and/or terminate or disallow extra good time (an extra good time or good conduct time sanction may not be suspended).
102 - Escape from escort; escape from a secure institution (low, medium, and high security level and administrative institutions); or escape from a minimum institution With violence.	B.1 Disallow ordinarily between 50 and 75% (27-41 days) of good conduct time credit available for year (a good conduct time sanction may not be suspended).
	C. Disciplinary Transfer (recommend).
	D. Disciplinary segregation (up to 60 days).
	E. Make monetary restitution.

29

CODE PROHIBITED ACTS	SANCTIONS
103 - Setting a fire (charged with this act in this category only when found to pose a threat to life or a threat of serious bodily harm or in furtherance of a prohibited act of Greatest Severity, i.e. in furtherance of a riot or escape; otherwise the charge is properly classified Code 218, or 329).	F. Withhold statutory good time (Note - can be in addition to A through E - cannot be the only sanction executed).
104 - Possession, manufacture or introduction of a gun, firearm, weapon, sharpened instrument, knife, dangerous chemical, explosive or any ammunition.	G. Loss of privileges (Note - can be in addition to A through E - cannot be the only sanction executed).
105 - Rioting.	
106 - Encouraging others to riot.	
107 - Taking hostage(s).	

CODE PROHIBITED ACTS	SANCTIONS
108 - Possession, manufacture or introduction of a hazardous tool (tools most likely to be used in a escape or escape attempt or to serve as weapons capable of doing serious bodily harm to others; or those hazardous to institutional security or personal safety; i.e., a hacksaw blade).	Sanctions A-G
109 - (Not to be used).	
110 - Refusing to provide a urine sample or to take part in other drug abuse testing.	
111 - Introduction of any narcotics, marijuana, drugs, or related paraphernalia not prescribed for the individual by the medical staff.	

CODE PROHIBITED ACTS	SANCTIONS
112 - Use of any narcotics, marijuana, drugs, or related paraphernalia not Prescribed for the individual by the medical staff. 113 - Possession of any narcotics, marijuana, drugs, or related paraphernalia not prescribed for the individual by the medical staff. 197 - Use of the telephone to further criminal activity. 198 - Interfering with a staff member in the performance of duties. (Conduct must be of the Greatest Severity nature.) This charge is to be used only when another charge of Greatest Severity is not applicable.	Sanctions A-G

CODE PROHIBITED ACTS	SANCTIONS
199 - Conduct which disrupts or interferes with the security or orderly running of the institution or the Bureau of Prisons. (Conduct must be of the Greatest Severity nature). This charge is to be used only when another charge of Greatest Severity is not applicable.	Sanctions A-G

HIGH CATEGORY

CODE PROHIBITED ACTS	SANCTIONS	
200 - Escape from unescorted community programs and activities, and open institutions (Minimum) and from outside secure institutions – without violence. 201 - Fighting with another person. 202 - (Not to be used). 203 - Threatening another with bodily harm or any other offence.	A.	Recommend parole date rescission or retardation
	B.	Forfeit earned statutory good time or non-vested good conduct time (up to 50%) or up to 60 days whichever is less, and/or terminate or disallow extra good time (an extra good time or good conduct time sanction may not be suspended).

CODE PROHIBITED ACTS	SANCTIONS
204 - Extortion, blackmail, protection: Demanding or receiving money or anything of value in return for protection against others, to avoid bodily harm, or under threat of informing.	B.1 Disallow ordinarily between 25 and 50% (14-27 days) of good conduct time credit available for year (a good conduct time sanction may not be suspended).
205 - Engaging in sexual acts.	C. Disciplinary Transfer (recommend).
206 - Making sexual proposals or threats to another.	D. Disciplinary segregation (Up to 30 days).
207 - Wearing a disguise of mask.	E. Make monetary restitution.
208 - Possession of any unauthorized locking device, or lock pick, or tampering with or blocking any locking device (includes keys), or destroying, altering, interfering with, improperly using or damaging any security device, mechanism, or procedure.	F. Withhold statutory good time.
	G. Loss of privileges: commissary, movies, recreation, etc..
	H. Change housing (quarters).
	I. Remove from program and/or group activity.
	J. Loss of job.
	K. Impound inmate's personal property.
	L. Confiscate contraband.
	M. Restrict to quarters

<u>CODE PROHIBITED ACTS</u>	<u>SANCTIONS</u>
209 - Alteration of any food or drink.	Sanctions A - M
210 - (Not to be used).	
211 - Possessing any officer's or staff clothing.	
212 - Engaging in, or encouraging a group demonstration.	
213 - Encouraging others to refuse to work, or to participate in a work stoppage.	
214 - (Not to be used).	
215 - Introduction of alcohol into a BOP facility.	
216 - Giving or offering an official or staff member a bribe, or anything of value.	
217 - Giving money to, or receiving money from, any person for purposes of introducing contraband or for any other illegal or prohibited purposes.	

CODE PROHIBITED ACTS	SANCTIONS
218 - Destroying, altering, or damaging government property, or the property of another person, having a value in excess of $100.00; or destroying, altering, damaging life-safety devices (e.g., fire alarm) regardless of financial value.	Sanctions A - M
219 - Stealing (theft; this includes data obtained through the unauthorized use of a communications facility, or through the unauthorized access to disk, tapes, or computer printouts or other automated equipment on which data is stored).	
220 - Demonstrating, practicing, or using martial arts, boxing (except for use of a punching bag), wrestling, or other form of physical, or military exercises or drills (except for drill authorized and conducted by staff).	

CODE PROHIBITED ACTS	SANCTIONS
221 - Being in an unauthorized area with a person of the opposite sex without staff permission.	Sanctions A - M
222 - Making, possessing, or using intoxicants.	
223 - Refusing to breathe into a breathalyser or take part in other testing for use of alcohol.	
224 - Assaulting any person (Charged with this act only when a less serious physical injury or contact has been attempted or carried out by an inmate).	
297 - Use of telephone for abuses other than criminal activity (e.g., circumventing telephone monitoring procedures, possession and/or use of another inmate's PIN number; third-party calling; third-party billing; using credit card numbers to place telephone calls; conference calling; talking in code).	

CODE PROHIBITED ACTS	SANCTIONS
298 - Interfering with a staff member in the performance of duties. (CONDUCT MUST BE OF THE HIGH SEVERITY NATURE). This charge is to be used only when another charge of the high severity is not applicable.	Sanctions A - M
299 - Conduct which disrupts or Interferes with the security or orderly running of the Bureau of Prisons (CONDUCT MUST BE OF THE HIGH SEVERITY NATURE). This charge is to be used only when another charge of high severity is not applicable.	

CODE PROHIBITED ACTS	SANCTIONS
300 - Indecent exposure.	A. Recommend parole date rescission or retardation.
301 - (Not to be used).	
302 - Misuse of authorized medication.	B. Forfeit earned statutory good time or non-vested good conduct time up to 25% or up to 30 days, whichever is less, and/or terminate or disallow extra good time (an extra good time or good conduct time sanction may not be suspended).
303 - Possession of money or currency, unless specifically authorized, or in excess of the amount authorized.	
304 - Loaning of property or anything of value for profit or increased return.	
305 - Possession of anything not authorized for retention or receipt by the inmate, and not issued to him through regular channels.	B.1 Disallow ordinarily up to 25% (1-14 days) of good conduct time credit available for year (a good conduct time sanction may not be suspended).
306 - Refusing to work, or to accept a program assignment.	
	C. Disciplinary Transfer (recommend).
	D. Disciplinary segregation (up to 15 days).
	E. Make monetary restitution.
	F. Withhold statutory good time.
	G. Loss of privileges: commissary, movies, recreation, etc..

CODE PROHIBITED ACTS	SANCTIONS
307 - Refusing to obey an order of any staff member (may be categorized and charged in terms of greater severity, according to the nature of the order being disobeyed; e.g., failure to obey an order which furthers a riot would be charged as 105, Rioting; refusing to obey an order which furthers a fight would be charged as 201, Fighting; refusing to provide a urine sample when ordered would be charged as code 110).	H. Change housing (quarters).
	I. Remove from program and/or group activity.
	J. Loss of job.
	K. Impound inmate's personal property.
	L. Confiscate contraband.
308 - Violating a condition of a furlough.	M. Restrict to quarters.
	N. Extra duty.
309 - Violating a condition of a community program.	
310 - Unexcused absence from work or any assignment.	
311 - Failing to perform work as instructed by a supervisor.	
312 - Insolence toward a staff member.	
313 - Lying or providing a false statement to a staff member.	

CODE PROHIBITED ACTS	SANCTIONS
314 - Counterfeiting, forging, or unauthorized reproduction of any document, articles of identification, money, security, or official paper (may be categorized in terms of Greatest Severity according to the nature of the item being reproduced, i.e., counterfeiting release papers to affect escape, Code 102 or Code 200).	Sanctions A - N
315 - Participating in an unauthorized meeting or gathering.	
316 - Being in an unauthorized area.	
317 - Failure to follow safety or sanitation regulations.	
318 - Using any equipment or machinery which is not specifically authorized.	
319 - Using any equipment or machinery contrary to instructions or posted safety standards.	
320 - Failing to stand for count.	
321 - Interfering with the taking of count.	
322 - (Not to be used).	

41

CODE PROHIBITED ACTS	SANCTIONS
323 - (Not to be used).	Sanctions A - N
324 - Gambling.	
325 - Preparing or conducting a gambling pool.	
326 - Possession of gambling paraphernalia.	
327 - Unauthorized contact with the public.	
328 - Giving money or anything of value to, or accepting money or anything of value from, another inmate or any other person without staff authorization.	
329 - Destroying, altering, or damaging government property, or the property of another person, having a value of $100.00 or less.	
330 - Being unsanitary or untidy; failing to keep one's person and other quarters in accordance with posted standards.	
331 - Possession, manufacture, or introduction of a nonhazardous tool or other nonhazardous contraband (a tool not likely to be used in an escape or escape attempt, or to serve as a weapon capable of doing serious bodily harms to others, or not hazardous to institutional	Sanctions A - N

CODE PROHIBITED ACTS	SANCTIONS	
400 - Possession of property belonging to another person.	B.1	Disallow ordinarily up to 12.5% (1-7 days) of good conduct time credit available for year (to be used only where inmate is found to have committed a second violation of the same prohibited act within 6 months); Disallow ordinarily up to 25% (1-14 days) of good conduct time credit available for year (to be used only where inmate found to have committed a third violation of the same prohibited act within 6 months) (a good conduct time sanction may not be suspended). (See Chapter 4, Page 16 for VCCLEA violent and PLRA inmates).
401 - Possessing unauthorized amounts of, otherwise, authorized clothing.		
402 - Malingering or feigning illness.		
403 - (Not to be used).		
404 - Using abusive or obscene language.		
405 - Tattooing or self-mutilation.		
406 - (Not to be used).		
407 - Conduct with a visitor in violation of Bureau regulations (Restriction, or loss for a specific period of time, of these privilege may often be an appropriate Sanction G).		
408 - Conducting a business.	C.	Make monetary restitution.
409 - Unauthorized physical contact (e.g., kissing, embracing).	D.	Withhold statutory good time.
	E.	Loss of privileges: commissary, movies, recreation, etc..
	F.	Confiscate contraband
	G.	Change housing (quarters).
	H.	Remove from program and/or group activity.

CODE PROHIBITED ACTS	SANCTIONS
410 - Unauthorized use of mail (restriction, or loss for a specific period of time, of these privileges may often be an appropriate Sanction G). (May be categorized and charged in terms of greater severity, according to the nature of the unauthorized use; e.g., the mail is used for planning, facilitating, committing an armed assault on the institution's secure perimeter, would be charged as Code 101, Assault). 497 - Use of the telephone for abuses other than criminal activity (e.g., exceeding the 15-minute time limit for telephones calls; using the telephone in an unauthorized area; placing of an unauthorized individual on the telephone list).	I. Loss of job. J. Impound inmate's personal property. K. Restrict to quarters. L. Extra duty. M. Reprimand. N. Warning.

CODE PROHIBITED ACTS	SANCTIONS
498 - Interfering with a staff member in the performance of duties. (CONDUCT MUST BE OF THE LOW MODERATE SEVERITY NATURE). This charge is to be used only when another charge of low moderate severity is not applicable. 499 - Conduct which disrupts or Interferes with the security or orderly running of the institution or the Bureau of Prisons. (CONDUCT MUST BE OF THE LOW MODERATE SEVERITY NATURE). This charge is to be used only when another charge of low moderate severity is not applicable.	Sanctions B.1 - P

NOTE:

Aiding another person to commit any of these offenses, attempting to commit any of these offenses, and making plans to commit any of these offenses, in all categories of severity, shall be considered the same as a commission of the offence itself.

When the prohibited act is interfering with a staff member in the performance of duties (Code 198, 298, 398, or 498), or Conduct Which Disrupts (Code 199, 299, 399, or 499), the DHO or UDC, in its findings, should indicate a specific finding of severity level of the conduct, and a comparison to an offense in that severity level which the DHO pr UDC finds is most comparable.

Inmates found in possession of an electronic communication device or related equipment may be charged with a violation of Code 108, Possession, Manufacture, or Introduction of a Hazardous Tool, or Code 199 most likely Code 108, and will be subject to available sanctions if found to have committed the prohibited act.

INMATE
RIGHTS AND RESPONSIBILITIES

RIGHTS	RESPONSIBILITIES
1. You have the right to expect that as a human being, you will be treated respectfully, impartially, and fairly by all personnel.	1. You have the responsibility to treat others, both employees and inmates, in the same manner.
2. You have the right to be informed of the rules, procedures, and schedules concerning the operation of the institution.	2. You have the responsibility to know and abide by them.
3. You have the right to freedom of religious affiliation and voluntary religious worship.	3. You have the responsibility to recognize and respect the rights of others in this regard.
4. You have the right to health care, which includes nutritious meals, proper bedding and clothing, and a laundry schedule for cleanliness of the same, an opportunity to shower regularly, proper ventilation for warmth and fresh air, a regular exercise period, toilet articles and medical and dental treatment.	4. It is Your responsibility not to waste food, to follow the laundry and shower schedule, maintain neat and clean living quarters, to keep your area free of contraband, and to seek medical and dental care as you may need it.
5. You have the right to visit and correspond with family members and friends, and correspond with members of the news media in keeping with Bureau rules and institution guidelines.	5. It is your responsibility to conduct yourself properly during visits; not to accept or pass contraband; and not to violate the law or Bureau rules, or institutional guidelines through your correspondence.

RIGHTS	RESPONSIBILITIES
6. You have the right to unrestricted and confidential access to the courts by correspondence (On matters such as the legality of your conviction, civil matters, pending criminal cases, and conditions of your imprisonment).	6. You have the responsibility to present honestly and fairly, your petitions, questions, and problems to the court.
7. You have the right to legal counsel from an attorney of your choice by interviews and correspondence.	7. It is your responsibility to use the services of an attorney honestly and fairly.
8. You have the right to participate in the use of the Law Library reference materials to assist you in resolving legal problems. You also have the right to receive help when it is available through a legal assistance program.	8. It is your responsibility to use these resources in keeping with the procedures and schedule prescribed and to respect the rights of other inmates as to the use of the materials and assistance.
9. You have the right to a wide range of reading material for educational purposes and for your own enjoyment. These materials may include magazines and newspapers sent from the community, with certain restrictions.	9. It is your responsibility to seek and utilize such materials for your personal benefit without depriving others of their equal rights to the use of this material.
10. You have the right to participate in education, vocational training and employment as far as resources are available, and in keeping with your interest, needs and abilities.	10. You have the responsibility to take advantage of activities which may help you live a successful and law-abiding life within the institution and in the community. You will be expected to abide by the regulations governing the use of such activities.

RIGHTS	RESPONSIBILITIES
11. You have the right to use your funds for Commissary and other purchases, consistent with institution security and good order, for opening bank and/or savings accounts, and for assisting your family.	11. You have the responsibility to meet your financial and legal obligations, including, but not limited to, court-imposed assessments, fines, and restitution. You also have the responsibility to make use of your funds in a manner consistent with your release plans, your family needs, and other obligations that you may have.

SPECIAL HOUSING UNIT
INMATE RULES

The following is a list of rules that shall be observed in The Special Housing Unit by all inmates assigned to either Administrative Detention or Disciplinary Segregation.

****

1. This is a non-smoking unit.

2. You will be allowed three (3) showers per week, normally on Sunday, Tuesday and Thursday.

3. You will be provided the opportunity for a minimum of five (5) hours of recreation/exercise a week. One (1) hour per day, Monday through Friday. All cells will be cleaned and beds made before inmates are allowed to go to recreation. All inmates will be dressed in the assigned uniform before being allowed to receive recreation.

4. **(A)** While in administrative detention status, you will be afforded the opportunity of one (1) phone call every seven (7) days, beginning from the time of your first call.

    (B) While in disciplinary segregation status, you will be afforded the opportunity of one (1) phone call every thirty (30) days, beginning from the time of your first call. All requests for phone calls must be submitted in writing and approved by the Special Housing Lieutenant.

5. Monday through Friday, the lights will be turned on at 6:00 a.m. You will be required to make up your bed and clean your cell prior to 7:30 a.m. Once this is completed, then you may lay on top of your bed.

6. You will not be allowed to hang anything on your cell wall, lights, window or bunks at any time. This includes blankets, sheets, clothing or anything else prohibiting staff from seeing into the cell.

7. Sick call is between 6:00 a.m. and 6:30 a.m., Monday through Friday.

8. The designated quiet hours in the unit are from 11:00 p.m. to 6:00 a.m. During this period, there will be no yelling or any other disruptive behavior which will disturb other inmates.

9. Inmate Request To Staff Member forms (cop-outs) are available from the officers on duty and should be used for all requests for staff.

49

10. You will be afforded the opportunity for hair cut, twice a month. All requests must be submitted, in writing, and directed to the SHU lieutenant.

11. You will be allowed to exchange unit issued linen, clothing and towels, once a week. Usually conducted on Tuesday.

12. You are only permitted to keep two (1) cups in your cell at any time.

13. All inmates will stand for the 4:00 p.m. and 10:00 a.m. (Weekend/Holiday) count.

NOTE:

Pursuant to Bureau of Prisons' Inmate Telephone Regulations: All conversations on this telephone are subject to monitoring. Your use of this telephone constitutes consent to this monitoring. You must contact your unit team to request an unmonitored Attorney call.

INMATE SYSTEMS MANAGEMENT (ISM)

Through the Inmate Systems Management Department (ISM), you not only enter on your first day, but you will also depart the facility (release, furlough, transfer, court appearance, etc.). Your mail, property, and, most important, your records are processed here. ISM is divided into three functional areas: Receiving and Discharge (R&D), Mail Room, and Record Office. There is an ISM Open House from 11:30 a.m. to 12:00 p.m. noon on Tuesdays and Thursdays to answer questions regarding your mail, property, prior custody credit, or sentence computation. Open House is held at the G Unit Grill Entrance to R&D.

Camp open house is on Thursdays at 10:30 a.m. until the end of Lunch.

R&D/PROPERTY MANAGEMENT:

Upon your arrival at this facility, you are allowed to keep only that property authorized by this institution.

When departing the facility, your property will be shipped to your destination or to an address of your choice. If property is not claimed and is returned to this facility, it will be considered abandoned and will be disposed of according to Bureau of Prisons procedures. Provisions may be made for the delivery of release clothing or court clothes, if needed. This will be arranged through your Unit Team.

Only one radio (battery operated), with inmate register number engraved as proof of ownership, and one watch, with Inmate Personal Property Record Form 383 and/or a commissary receipt as proof of ownership, may be retained. The radio may not be equipped with taping capability, must be equipped with earphone adaptor and must not exceed $75.00 in value. The watch may not exceed $100.00 in value.

A religious medal and chain, inclusive value of not more than $100.00, may be possessed. All questions regarding religious articles will be referred to the Chaplain.

Any article that is not issued to you, purchased by you from the commissary, or for which you do not have authorization, is contraband. Articles of clothing in excess of allowed limits and articles used for unauthorized purposes are also considered contraband. Possession of contraband is a serious offence and can result in disciplinary action.

MAIL ROOM/CORRESPONDENCE:

INCOMING mail is processed by ISM Staff. All general correspondence is opened and inspected for contraband. Correspondence from attorneys will be treated as Special Mail (delivered by Mail Room Staff, opened and inspected in the presence of the inmate) if it is properly marked. The envelope must be marked with the attorney's name and an indication that he or she is an attorney. The front of the envelope must be marked "**Special Mail - Open Only in the Presence of the Inmate**." It is the responsibility of the inmate to advise his attorney about this policy. If legal mail is not properly marked, it will be opened as general correspondence.

Newspapers and magazines may be received on a regular basis by subscription and must be receive directly from the publisher.

You may receive hardcover books from a publisher, book club or book store. You are limited to five books, two current magazines and one current newspaper in your possession at any time. Education or Religious materials for ongoing courses are exempt from this requirement.

The following items may not be mailed into the institution:

    1.Postage Stamps.

    2.Stationery Supplies.

    3.Unused Greeting Cards, including the Small Plastic Cards.

4.Musical Greeting Cards.

5.Nude Photographs (Including Magazines).

6.Polaroid Pictures.

First-class mail and publications are distributed Monday through Friday, excluding holidays, after the 4:00 P.M. count. Inmates are required to attend mail call. All mail received from the U.S. Post Office is normally processed for delivery the same day it arrives.

The **ONLY** authorized express service for approved packages and letter receipt is via U.S. Postal Service Express Mail. Express Mail received for inmates is processed as first-class mail upon receipt at the institution. Mail from Federal Express, United Parcel Service, and like companies is not accepted for delivery to inmates.

An authorization must be on file in the Mail Room prior to a package arrival at the institution. If there is no authorization, the package will be refused at the U.S. Post Office and returned to sender. A copy of the signed authorization must be enclosed inside the package. Authorization may be obtained from the appropriate department, the Unit Team, the Chaplain, Education, or Health Services.

OUTGOING:

General correspondence will be deposited in the mailbox located in the housing units. Outgoing mail may be sealed. Special mail (legal mail) for inmates may be dropped off in the Lieutenant's office during the following times:

Monday thru Friday 7:00 a.m. to 7:15 a.m.

Saturday - Sunday and Federal holidays 9:00 a.m to 9:15 a.m., which may be sealed. Express mail and C.O.D. services are not available for inmate outgoing mail.

All mail addressed to or from an inmate must contain the following information:

> **Committed Name**
> **Register Number**
> **Federal Correctional Institution**
> **P.O. Box 779800**
> **Miami, Florida 33177**

All outgoing inmate mail will display an appropriate return address in the upper left-hand corner of the envelope. This will include the full name of the facility as "Federal Correctional Institution" and not the acronym "FCI." Any outgoing mail that does not contain the appropriate return address will be return to the inmate for correction.

Correspondence between confined federal inmates requires the approval of the Unit Manager at each institution. Correspondence between inmates at non-federal facilities requires the approval of the Warden at each institution. An inmate may correspond with family members or co-defendants (ongoing legal action in which both parties are involved) at other penal or correctional institution after this information has been verified by your unit team. To request this communication a cop out should be submitted to your unit team.

RECORD OFFICE:

This office is responsible for the legal commitment and release of offenders. Newly committed offenders will receive a sentence computation with a projected release date once it is completed. This normally occurs within thirty days of your arrival at the institution. For those inmates who transfer in from other institution, a new computation sheet will not necessarily be sent to you if there is no change in your projected release date.

Offenses committed after September 13, 1994 will be subject to the Violent Crime Control and law Enforcement Act and will be determined by Case Management to be either violent or non-violent. Offenses committed after April

26, 1996 will be subject to the Prison Litigation Reform Act. Both of these laws affect the discipline policy and the award, disallowance, and/or forfeiture of good conduct time.

INSTITUTION RELEASE PREPARATION PROGRAM

The Institution Release Preparation Program is a volunteer program for inmates who are within 30 months of release. Inmates will be recommended to participate in a core curriculum of programs that will focus on making the transition from incarceration to the community. Topics included in this core curriculum are organized into six broad categories such as Health and Nutrition, Employment, Personal Finance and Consumer Skills, Personal Growth and Development, Release Requirements and Procedures, and Community Resources (Pre-Release). Each course is outlined in a yearly calendar of classes offered at a minimum quarterly. Inmates may sign up for participation by submitting and "Inmate Request to Staff" to the department responsible for the course, and they will be placed on callout for the initial class. The goal of the program is to assist inmates in preparing for a successful release back into the community. This can be achieved when inmates release with job readiness skills, a resume', and finances saved for release purposes. Your Unit Team will discuss each of these areas during your regularly scheduled programs reviews. You will be referred for Institution Pre-Release when you are within one year of release.

This will allow you to ask questions of the U.S. Probation Office, Community Corrections Manager and Halfway House staff as well as, Social Security. Each inmate should develop a release folder during the last 24 months of incarceration to include a resume' and cover letter, all certificates of achievement, your education transcript, and sample applications for employment, and a copy of your social security card or appropriate photo ID.

Your Participation will be evaluated by your unit team during regularly scheduled program reviews. As with any program, you are held responsible to sigh up and participate.

This concept is somewhat new to the Bureau of Prisons but it is ultimately aimed at increasing your chance of securing stable employment upon release as well as developing healthy relationships with your family.

LAUNDRY

It is the policy of this institution to provide each inmate with an adequate issuance of clothing items, linens and bedding material, and to maintain an effective procedure for the laundering and exchange of those items. The hours for the Laundry are from 6:00 A.M. until 2:30 P.M., Monday thru Friday, (except Federal Holidays).

LAUNDERING PROCEDURES:

Clothing requiring laundering (except the Special Housing Unit) is accepted at the laundry window from 6:30 until 7:30 A.M., Monday, Wednesday and Friday. Inmates will drop off dirty institutional clothing only (khaki pants and shirts, T-shirts, underwear and socks) at the above mentioned times and days. All clothing must be inside the issued laundry bag identified with the bin number. It will be picked up the same day during the lunch hour. Non-institutional (personal) clothing will not be laundered.

Note:

Personal clothing is to be washed in the machines located in the housing units, NOT in the institution laundry. More detailed information can be found in the Institution Supplement on Inmate Personal Property.

Newly committed inmates will report to the laundry on their first day, from 6:30 to 7:30 A.M., to request their initial issuance of clothing. At that time, an order form will be completed by laundry staff. Clothes will be issued during the lunch hour of the same day.

REPLACEMENT PROCEDURES:

Inmates needing assistance with laundry issues should contact the laundry staff via "Inmate Request to Staff," stating their problem. Don't forget to include your laundry **BIN** number on the "Inmate Request to Staff."

Work clothing will be issued to those inmates who require special clothing for work details. Food Service clothing shall be delivered, for cleaning, on Tuesdays and Thursdays between 6:30 and 7:00 A.M. and picked up the same day during the lunch hour.

Washers and Dryers are available in each unit for those inmates who prefer to launder their clothes, at the cost of $0.50 to wash and $0.50 to dry. Those washers and dryers are **not** intended to be used to wash linens.

Linen exchange is the responsibility of each inmate. Each inmate must bring dirty linen to the laundry during clothing exchange hours at the laundry window (Mondays, Wednesdays and Fridays from 6:30 to 7:30 AM). Linen (blanket, sheets and pillow cases) **must** be exchanged regularly. Partial linen exchanges will not be allowed. All issued clothing, linen, towels, etc., are exchanged on a one-for-one basis.

CAMP LAUNDRY:
Camp inmates are responsible for washing their own linen while at the camp. There are no exchanges at the camp.

Camp laundry hours:

Tuesdays and Thursdays from 1:00 p.m. to 3:00 p.m.

Clothing issues to new commits, SHU releases and Writ returns to the Camp will be Monday through Friday, 6:30 am to 1:30 pm, if Laundry staff are available.

The first week of each month laundry detergent and hygiene packs are issued to the Camp population from 6:00 am to 1:00 pm.

The use of laundry issued items for cleaning/sanitation purposes will not be tolerated. Violators will be subject to disciplinary action.

PARALEGAL ISSUES
Attorney Representatives

28 C.F.R. 543.16 et seq.
Program Statement 1315.07
Institution Supplement MIA-1315.6-1A

These are individuals who are employed by duly licensed attorneys to perform specific task concerning your case. Investigators, interns, paralegals, and legal assistants fall into this category. The attorney for whom they work must authorize them to correspond, visit, and interview clients on their behalf. This authorization includes completion of an Application to Enter an Institution as Representative of an Attorney form. This application can be obtained by the attorney through a request to the institution's Management Analyst. Once completed, the attorney by whom the representative is employed, will verify the application and returned to the institution's Management Analyst for further processing.

The application must be accompanied with a pledge to supervise the representative's activities, and acceptance of personal and professional responsibility for all acts of the representative which may affect the institution, its inmates, and staff.

At least one (1) week, from the time the application and documentation is received, must be given for the processing of the application. When the application is cleared, the originals will remain on file. The representative will be allowed to correspond, visit and interview clients of the attorney for whom he/she works, however, at least 24 hours notice must be provided before each requested visit.

ADMINISTRATIVE REMEDIES

28 C.F.R. 542.10
Program Statement 1330.13
Institution Supplement MIA-1330.13B

If you cannot resolve a complaint through normal contact with staff, or through an "Inmate Request to Staff Member" form and wish to file a formal complain for administrative remedy, you must first attempt informal resolution through your unit Counselor. Documentation of your attempt must be attached to the formal "Request for Administrative Remedy" form when you return it for acceptance.

The "Request for Administrative Remedy" form is also obtain from a member of your unit team. The formal complain must be filed within twenty (20) calendar days on which the basis of the complaint occurred. You may only submit one complaint per form and the Warden has twenty (20) calendar days from receipt of the complaint to act upon the matter and provide a written response. A member of your unit team will provide you with a received which indicates the date your request was received and when the Warden's response is due.

If you are not satisfied with the Warden's response, you may file an appeal within twenty (20) calendar days to the Southeast Regional Director. This should be done on the proper "Request for Administrative Remedy Appeal" form and include a copy of the Warden's response as well as the "Request for Administrative Remedy" form you originally submitted.

This form can be obtain from a member of your unit team. The Regional Director has thirty (30) days upon receipt of your appeal to respond. Again, your unit Counselor will provide you with a receipt which indicates the date your request was received at the Regional level and when the Regional Director's response is due.

If you are not satisfied with this reply, you may file a final appeal to the Bureau of Prisons, Assistant Director, Office of General Counsel, within thirty (30) calendar days of receipt of the Regional Director's response. This must be done on the proper "Central Office Request for Administrative Appeal" form and must include a copy of the previous request and appeal with the responses. Within forty (40) calendar days, written response will be made.

As the procedures above note, your unit Counselor will provide you with a receipt which indicates the date your appeal was received at the Central Office level and the date the response is due.

The Management Analyst is the Administrative Remedy Coordinator at this institution. Should you have any questions, or experience difficulty with your Administrative Remedies, direct an "Inmate Request to Staff Member" form to the Management Analyst's attention.

Federal Tort Claims Act

28 U.S.C. 2671
28 C.F.R. 543.30
Program Statement 1320.03
Institution Supplement 1320.3C

The above mentioned statues and policies govern this type of claim where an inmate's personal property is lost or destroyed or an inmate receives personal injury caused by wrongful or negligent acts or failure of a government employee to act within the scope of his/her employment. The claim must be presented in writing with the supporting documentation to the Regional Office where the incident occurred.

In case of property loss, a copy of all documentation including proof of ownership, purchase, etc., must be included with the claim. This form can be obtained from the Business Office or through your Unit Team.

The statute of limitations requires the filing of an administrative claim within (2) years of the incident and requires the filing of a civil suit within six (6) months from the denial of the administrative claim (see your Unit Team or write an "Inmate Request to Staff Member" to the institution's Management Analyst for more details).

PERSONAL PROPERTY

Inmates are authorized to possess items, which are purchased in the Commissary, approved by the Warden, or authorized to be received by the inmate. The amount of property allowed (civilian or institution issue) will be limited to those items which can be neatly and safely stored inside their individual locker. Property that cannot be properly stored will be considered excess property, confiscated and disposed of according to current policy.

No inmate may be in possession of or authorize to retain dark blue, black, red, or camouflage clothing with the exception of American Indians as authorized by the Chaplain. No logos or slogans are permitted on inmates personal clothing.

Inmates will be held accountable for all property found in their lockers. You must maintain only authorized limits. Altered clothing will be considered contraband and disciplinary action may result.

For the **Authorized List and Limits** of personal property refer to the most recent copy of the Institution Supplement on Inmate Personal Property.

PRIVACY ACT

PRIVACY ACT OF 1974:
Forbids the release of information from agency records without a written request by, or prior written consent of, the individual to whom the record pertains, except in specific instances. Such specific instances are requests from employees of the Department of Justice, Law Enforcement Agencies, Freedom of Information Act Releases, Congress, Court Orders, etc..

ACCESS TO CENTRAL FILES

An inmate at any time may request to review all "disclosure portions" of his central files by submitting a request to his Unit Team. Staff will acknowledge the request and schedule the inmate, as promptly as possible, for a review of his file. The Freedom of Information Act (FOLA) Exempt section contains information that is not disclosable to you by Institution staff. You may request disclosure through writing Freedom of Information/Privacy Act (FOLA) Section, 320 First Street, NW, NALC Building, Room 401, Washington, D.C. 20534.

An inmate may request personal copies of central file documents. Institution staff will arrange for copies of disclosable materials and summaries. Fees are charged in accordance with 28 CFR 16.46. Fees collected will be forwarded to the Office of General Counsel

PSYCHOLOGY SERVICES

The Department of Psychology at FCI-Miami identifies and treats inmates with mental health problems. As part of their functions, the department helps inmates cope with difficulties that surface as a result of incarceration and separation from home, family, and friends. The psychology and medical staff work closely together to provide a coordinated approach to treatment. The psychology department also conducts psychological evaluations, provides crisis consultation, makes referrals to Medical Services, and offers individual and group counseling. Services in English and Spanish.

The Psychology Department provides a 40-hour comprehensive, voluntary, treatment program for individuals with a history of drug or alcohol use. Groups are available to educate the inmate population on the effects of drug use, as well as to provide support for those recovering from their drug use. Details of these meetings are available from the Drug Abuse Program Coordinator and/or the Drug Treatment Specialist, Monday through Friday (excluding holidays). Inmates requiring individual counseling sessions can request these by submitting a cop-out.

The Residential Drug Abuse Treatment Program consists of 500 intensive treatment hours during which the inmate explores the factors that contributed to his use of drugs and alcohol, and the effect of such decision on his life. To apply for this program the inmate needs to prove a history of drug/alcohol abuse, cannot have a history of violence in his background, and needs to be an American citizen (or Cuban national).

Incentives of the RDAP: Certain inmates may be eligible for six-month CCC placement and a sentence reduction of up to 12 months upon successful completion of RDAP and community transitional services. In order to be eligible for these incentives, the inmate must first be deemed qualified to participate in RDAP. Inmates will be notified in writing regarding their eligibility for early release. If you are interested in participating in this program or obtaining additional information to determine if you are eligible, please submit a cop-out.

The "I CAN" is a residential program for inmates interested in changing those behaviors, thoughts, attitudes, that are conducive to criminal behavior and recidivism. Each participant is required to take a set of core courses (7 Habits of Highly Effective People, Living Free, Errors in Criminal Thinking, Goal Setting, Empowering Your Thinking) along with numerous classes offered throughout the institution and on the Unit.

Inmates interested in receiving psycho-educational material over the radio can do so by tuning in to station 107.9. While on this channel, inmates will be exposed to a diverse series of lectures that include topics such as principles for success, self-awareness, a balanced life, basic financial principles, among others.

D.C Inmates: DC Code offenders may possibly be eligible for early release consideration who become involved in the RDAP. This effects only D.C. Code felony offenders sentenced under § 24-403.01, for an offense committed on or after August 5, 2000. Please contact psychology staff for further information.

The Suicide Watch Companion Program is a component of the Suicide Prevention Program. Participants in this program observe suicidal inmates placed who have been placed on Suicide Watch. Furthermore, The Inmate Speakers Program involves a select group of inmates who speak to high school students on the perils of a life of crime

The Psychology Department recognizes that some inmates would like to discontinue employing products containing tobacco. The Psychology Department offers a Smoking Cessation Program which emphasizes healthy living, including nutrition, exercise, and stress management. Nicotine replacement patches are available for purchase through the institution commissary once an inmate has been cleared by Health Services to receive this intervention. For information about nicotine replacement therapy, please submit an Inmate Request to Staff to the Health Services Department. For all other information about smoking cessation, please submit and Inmate Request to Staff form to the Psychology Department

Psychology Services, along with medical, unit, and correctional staff are here to ensure your safety from sexual abuse. Any inmate who is the victim of a sexual abuse and/or assault is advised to notify any staff member immediately. Sexual abusive behavior is defined as any of the following behaviors:

> sexual fondling - the touching of the private body parts of another person (including the genitalia, anus, groin, breast, inner thigh, or buttocks) for the purpose of sexual gratification.

> sexual assault with an object - the use of any hand, finger, object, or other instrument to penetrate, however slightly, the genital or anal opening of the body of another person

> rape - the carnal knowledge, oral sodomy, or sexual assault with an object or sexual fondling of a person forcibly or against the person's will; the carnal knowledge, oral sodomy, or sexual assault with an object or sexual fondling of a person not forcibly or against the person's will where the victim is incapable of giving consent because of his/her youth or his/her temporary or permanent mental or physical incapacity

Several prevention strategies inmates can take to minimize his risk of sexual victimization include: awareness of others who cross inappropriate boundaries; reinforcing personal boundaries; avoiding individuals who offer excessive favors, avoiding sexual acting out (e.g., swatting someone on the buttocks).

If you wish to report an incident of sexually abusive behavior, or wish to report allegations of sexually abusive behavior involving other inmates, all you need to do is bring the behavior to the attention of staff.

Lastly, to access psychology staff submit a cop-out or come by the department to ask for an appointment.

RECREATION DEPARTMENT

Our Recreation Department offers a large variety of programs and activities designed to meet the needs and demands of all inmates, varying in age, physical abilities and cultural backgrounds.

It is our goal to create a more active and healthier inmate population through regular participation in our programs and activities. The Recreation Department strongly encourages participation in its available structured, unstructured and/or spectator programs and activities. Operating hours for the recreation yard are listed below. Recreation personnel are available to provide assistance in planning and coordinating holiday programming and special events.

STRUCTURED PROGRAMS:
These include all types of cultural, social, recreational and creative activities that enrich life and stimulate development.
They are designated to enhance day to day activities of individual inmates and to serve various needs.

UNSTRUCTURED & SPECTATOR ACTIVITIES:
Includes social interaction and constructive leisure-time programs. These activities accommodate diverse needs and a wide range of age groups.

They encourage special interest, develop leadership and self -reliance, influence individual skills and communication capability.

RECREATION YARD SCHEDULE

Hours of operation and recreation programs are subject to change based on: security, staffing, inclement weather, lighting, etc.

WEEKDAYS

6:00 A.M.	— Recreation Yard Opens (Weather Permitting)
10:00 A.M.	— Rec. Yard closes (Except Wednesday 9:00 a.m.)
10:40 A.M.	— Rec. Yard opens
3:30 P.M.	— Rec. Yard\Bldg. Closes
4:30 P.M.	— Rec. Yard\Bldg. Opens
DUSK	— Outer Rec. Yard
8:30 P.M.	— Inner Rec. Yard/Bldg. Closes

WEEKENDS AND HOLIDAYS

7:00A.M.	— Recreation Yard Opens (Weather Permitting)
9:30A.M.	— Rec. Yard closes
10:30A.M.	— Rec. Yard opens (Pending Count)
3:30P.M.	— Rec. Yard\Bldg. Closes
4:30P.M.	— Rec. Yard\Bldg. Opens
DUSK	— Outer Rec. Yard
8:30P.M.	— Inner Rec. Yard/Bldg. Closes

CAMP RECREATION YARD HOURS

From Sunrise to Sundown (Year round)

RELIGIOUS SERVICES

A full program of Religious Services and meetings for inmates of all religious faiths is provided. Please check bulletin boards in the Chapel and in the units for a weekly schedule of religious activities. The schedule will indicate the duty hours that the Chaplain is available to provide pastoral care, counseling, and assist with emergency notices. Worship Services are also posted. A full-time Chaplain is on duty to care for the spiritual needs of inmates, regardless of religious or denominational affiliation. Worship opportunities and educational experiences are available to a variety of faith groups are available to provide assistance to inmates. Attendance at all religious functions is voluntary.

The Chaplain is available for consultation on common fare religious diet, religious property, marriage application, and emergency notifications of serious illness or death, attendance at religious holy days.

SAFETY

The Safety Office is responsible for the Safety and Occupational Health Program here at FCI Miami. It is the mission of the Safety Department to maintain a clean and safe living environment. The following regulations and procedures will be strictly enforced. Any questions concerning these regulations and procedures will be directed immediately to the attention of the Safety Manager.

FIRE SAFETY:

Is a critical area of concern to all persons staff and/or inmate, therefore the Safety Department continually monitors the entire facility for areas which may pose a fire threat. Daily, weekly and monthly inspections are conducted of all living and work areas for fire hazards.

Fire protection equipment consists of portable fire extinguishers, heat and smoke detectors with audible alarms and automatic sprinkler systems. Any person or persons responsible for tampering or damaging fire protection equipment will be subject to disciplinary action as well as possible criminal prosecution.

All fire and evacuation plans are posted in English and Spanish. Upon assignment to a housing unit and work detail, you should become familiar with each plan, emergency exits and assembly area for each location.

To ensure that both, staff and inmates know exactly what to do in case of a fire, quarterly fire drills are conducted in all areas of the institution.

FIRE DRILL AND EMERGENCY EVACUATION PROCEDURES:

All departments conduct a fire drill once a quarter. Housing units conduct a fire drill on each shift once a year. When a fire drill is announced, you must:

1. Stop what you are doing.
2. Turn off machinery or equipment; set down your tools.
3. Quietly leave the building in the direction instructed. If a specific exit or direction is not identified, evacuate to the closest exit.
4. Assemble in a safe location and wait for further instructions.

During an emergency, cooperate with staff instructions and promptly evacuate the area. Avoid heavy smoke that rises to the ceiling by staying low; crawl to the nearest exit if necessary.

HAZARDOUS COMMUNICATION PLAN:

Chemicals are used for cleaning and maintenance at this facility. You will receive training on chemicals if you are assigned to a detail where chemicals are used. This training is called chemical hazard communication and will cover necessary precautions to prevent injury.

If you have any questions or concerns about chemical products in this facility, please refer to the product label or direct your concerns to a supervisor. Using or disposing of a product contrary to the label is prohibited and could result in disciplinary action.

This facility is registered under the United States Environmental Protection Agency (EPA), as a small generator of hazardous waste. This institution as a whole does not generate more than 80 kilograms of hazardous waste per month. Currently, this waste is limited to pain thinner, lacquer thinner, motor oil and solvent from the print shop. All hazardous wastes are legally and safely stored for disposal in the hazardous waste storage site located at the institution garage.

We meet all requirements by Federal Law under the Environmental Protection Agency, State of Florida and Dade County Environmental Resource Management (DERM). Weekly and monthly inspections are conducted and maintained and all reporting requirements are met.

In addition, as a worker assigned to a particular detail, you may be subject to using, mixing or applying chemical substances as part of your daily work functions. In such cases, all inmates must be familiar with all materials that may be used in their work site. Accordingly, you are to be familiar with the Material Safety Data Sheet (MSDS) for every substance that you work with.

The MSDS provides a detailed printout of all pertinent information of any chemical product which you may use in the course of your work. It will also provide you with what type of Personal Protective Equipment is needed if any. Should you became aware of, or believe that a specific hazardous condition exists, contact the Safety Department immediately via your supervisor or any staff member.

HAZARDOUS REPORTING PROCEDURES:

Notify the Safety Department by use of an "Inmate Request to Staff Member" (COP-OUT) form if you have any questions or concerns. You may also obtain a pass from your detail supervisor to visit our office. The Safety Department is located directly behind the Commissary Building.

INJURIES AND INMATE ACCIDENT COMPENSATION

Unless you are medically unassigned, you will be assigned to a work detail. Regardless of where you are assigned you are required and held accountable to follow basic safety regulations.

BP169:

Inmate Accident Compensation Handbook. You are required to sign a receipt (form **BP169**) stating you have read this form and received a copy of the Inmate Accident Compensation Handbook. This form is an acknowledgment that you have been advised of your right to file for compensation should you sustain a work related injury while incarcerated.

A work related injury is defined as an injury sustained while in the performance of maintaining a Federal Correctional Institution. Horseplay, fighting or recreational activities are not covered.

Under Part 301, Chapter III, of Title 28CFR, you must report any work related injury immediately to your work supervisor or any staff member. Upon notification, your supervisor or staff member will direct you to the Health Services Department for examination and/or treatment. An injury accident report will be filed and maintained in the Safety Department.

Should your injury result in you being unable to work for more than three working days, you are entitled to be paid for those days at 75% of the amount of pay held prior to the injury.

If you received a permanent injury, a claim for compensation cannot be filed until 45 days from your official release from federal custody, regardless of the type of release or your INS deportation status. To file your claim you must do so with the Safety Department. You must complete BP S658.016 and a final examination will be scheduled to determine the extent of your disability. All forms will be sent to the Central Office, Washington, D.C. for review and final adjudication.

SANITATION

There are several reasons why each Federal Correctional Facility requires a high level of sanitation, and the mandatory cooperation of each individual inmate in maintaining this level.

However, the most important factors include maintaining a level of sanitation which affords a clean and safe atmosphere in order to assist in the reduction or elimination of unnecessary accidents, decrease occurrences of pest infestation, control the spread of communicable diseases and provide an overall atmosphere in which work and living areas are environmentally safe and free of hazards.

It is the responsibility of each inmate in a room to maintain a high standard of sanitation at all times. All rooms will have a daily sanitation inspection. Failure to attain a satisfactory sanitation rating may result in disciplinary action. The following instructions are a guide to assist inmates in maintaining their individual room areas on a daily basis. The requirements will be met for room sanitation on a daily basis:

Common Areas:
Each individual inmate has a responsibility for the maintenance and sanitation of all common areas, such as, outside area, showers, dormitory bathrooms and TV viewing areas. Each inmate should leave these areas as they would like to find them.

At no time will any changes be made in any inmate living area to any physical plant structure or fixtures that may cause harm or injury to themselves or others. Inmates should inspect their own living areas and follow all stated guidelines listed. If there are any problems which need to be corrected, report these to the appropriate staff member.

Personal Property:
All personal property will be maintained in amounts permitted by policy and will be maintained in a neat and orderly manner at all times. The following are requirements for specific personal items:

Sanitation is a major area of concern in the Bureau of Prisons and will be strictly enforce at this institution. A clean living area reflects positively on the inmate population. Each unit will have orderlies assigned who are expected to keep the common areas of the unit clean.

Overall Room Appearance:
You must maintain your assigned area in an overall appearance that is clean and orderly at all times. At other times, inmates may lay in beds on top of the bedding, as long as the bed maintains a neat and a well-made appearance.

Bedding:
Will be washed frequently as to maintain good sanitation and hygiene in inmate living areas.

Furniture:
In rooms will be free of all stains, dirt, and are to be dusted daily.

Walls:
The walls in the room areas are to be kept clean and stain free on a daily basis, this includes any fixtures in this area. No items will be placed, taped or otherwise affixed to any wall surface or fixture in any cubicle area.

Light Fixtures:
Light bulbs or fixtures are not to be painted or covered in any way. Nothing will be hung from any electrical fixture or appliance.

Floors and Baseboards:
Are to be free of dust and dirt. Daily sweeping and mopping to maintain a clean surface is required.

Trash Containers:
Are to be emptied and cleaned on a daily basis. No plastic bags or liners are permitted.

Air Vents:
Must be cleaned on a daily basis.

Regardless of work assignment, you are responsible for keeping your living quarters clean at all times. Sanitation supplies are available in each unit. Those individuals who refuse or neglect to maintain an acceptable level of sanitation will be subject to disciplinary action.

PEST CONTROL OPERATION

The Pest Control operation of this institution is maintained by the Safety Department. Report all pest problems to the unit officer. A high level of sanitation will avoid pest problems. If you have problems with any pest or insects a Pest Control form must be filed with Safety Department.

ENVIRONMENTAL REGULATIONS AND PROCEDURES

1. It is the responsibility of each inmate worker to use the safety equipment issued to protect themselves against physical injury and/or health hazards. Make certain you have all required personal protective equipment on properly, such as goggles, safety shoes, aprons, arm guards, hard hats, and respirators, before you begin working.

2. You must wear safety goggles when performing any grinding, chiseling, filing, chipping, or buffing operations.

3. Safety Shoes are required by every inmate who works in the following areas: Food Service (All Areas), Unicor (All Areas), Commissary, Safety, Correctional Services Detail, Trash Detail and Recreation. Toe Caps and Foot Guards are Prohibited in the BOP.

4. Report all safety hazards immediately to your work supervisor. Do not continue to work in any area or on any machinery or equipment that is unsafe or improperly guarded. If your work supervisor does not agree that an unsafe condition exists, the fact should be reported to the institution Safety Manager.

5. Inmate employees will only perform work that is assigned to their operating machines. Performing any operation that has not been specifically assigned is strictly forbidden and may result in disciplinary action.

6. Operating the equipment without the safety guards provided or removal of the safety guards is forbidden and subject to disciplinary action.

7.   The fabrication or repair of personal items on government equipment (except when authorized in the hobby shop) is against safety regulations and prohibited. Do not try to adjust, oil, clean, repair, or perform any maintenance on any machine while in motion. Stop the machine if safe to do so and notify a staff member immediately. At no time will an inmate work on any type of energized equipment or circuits.

8.   Do not participate in weight lifting activities until authorized by the medical department. Safety shoes are recommended when participating in weigh lifting.

9.   Do not ride on the draw bars of vehicles. The operator is the only person authorized to ride on a tractor, forklift, or tow vehicle.

10. Do not stand up on moving vehicles. Sit on seats provided and where applicable, keep chains across the back in place. Do not attempt to dismount until the vehicle has completely stopped.
     Seat belts must be worn at all times when operating or riding in a government vehicle. Seat belts must also be worn when operating a forklift.

11. Inmate(s) who are injured while performing their assigned duties will immediately report such injury to their work supervisor (staff member). Failure to report a work injury to your supervisor within a maximum of 48 hours may disqualify you from eligibility for lost time, wages and compensation.

12. It is the responsibility of each inmate worker to exercise care, cooperation, and common sense in conducting assigned work. Horseplay on the job will not be tolerated. Any injury resulting from willful violation of rules and regulations may prevent an award of compensation.

13. Any inmate who sustains a work injury and still retains some degree of impairment at the same time of release should contact the Safety Manager not less than thirty (30) days prior to release or transfer to a CCC, for the purpose of submitting a claim for compensation. This claim must include a medical evaluation before any compensation can be considered.

14. All fire alarms/fire drills are to be adhered to at this facility. Failure to follow these rules, could result in disciplinary action against you.

15. Radios are forbidden on job sites and when operating any type of equipment or vehicle.

RECYCLING PROGRAM

The recycling program at FCI Miami at the present time includes: Cardboard, Aluminum Cans and White Paper. In the near future we plan on recycling Newspaper. This program can only work with the cooperation of all inmates. This will help in keeping the environment a cleaner and safer place to live.

SECURITY PROCEDURES
CONTRABAND

Contraband is defined as any item that is **NOT**:

1. Purchased through the commissary.
2. Authorized or issued by the institution, received through approved channels.
3. Permitted for retention.
4. Within the authorized limits.

Any staff member may search an inmate, property or living area at any time. It is not necessary for the inmate to be present during a cell search. Each inmate is responsible for all items found in their assigned living area. Keep records of the receipt of the items for proof authorization.

Radios will be marked with the inmate's register number at the time of purchase and/or approval for possession. You are NOT authorized to purchase radios or any other items from another inmate; items of this nature are considered contraband and will be confiscated. It is a violation of the institution's rules to lend or give your property to another inmate. Altered items, even if approved or issued is considered contraband. Altering or damaging government property is a violation of institutional rules and the cost of the damage will be levied against the violator.

CONTROLLED MOVEMENTS

Controlled Movement means that inmates are allowed a specific time (10 minutes) to move, from one point to another, within the institution. The times for movement are as follows:

WEEK DAYS	WEEKENDS AND HOLIDAYS
6:00 - 7:00 A.M. — Breakfast	7:00 A.M. — Coffee and Doughnuts
7:30 - 7:40 A.M. — Work Call	**(Open Movement on Weekends & Holidays)**
7:55 - 8:05 A.M. — Movement	7:55 - 8:05 A.M. — Movement
8:55 - 9:05 A.M. — Movement	8:55 - 9:05 A.M. — Rec. Move
9:55 - 10:05 A.M. — Movement	9:45-10:00 A.M. — Close Compound
10:45 A.M. — Noon meal starts *	10:00 A.M. — Official count
12:30 P.M. — Detail count (Approx.)	
12:55 - 1:05 P.M. — Movement	12:55 - 1:05 P.M. — Movement
1:55 - 2:05 P.M. — Movement	1:55 - 2:05 P.M. — Movement
2:55 - 3:05 P.M. — Movement	2:55 - 3:05 P.M. — Movement
3:30 P.M. — Pill Line/CMS release	3:30 P.M. — Pill line start
4:00 P.M. — Official count	4:00 P.M. — Official count
4:30 P.M. — Evening Meal starts	4:30 P.M. — Same
4:30-8:30 P.M. — Open Movement	4:30 -8:30 P.M. — Same
8:30 P.M. — Pill line starts	8:30 P.M. — Same
8:45 P.M. — Close compound	8:45 P.M. — Same
9:00 P.M. — Institutional Count Starts	9:00 P.M. — Same

There is no controlled movement at the camp.

Noon Meal Rotation:

Inmates are afforded thirty (30) minutes to eat and return to their assigned detail area. Inmates will be allowed to enter their assigned unit during lunch break if the unit was released for lunch, only. The compound will remain open for use during all meals.

COUNTS

To ensure accountability of all inmates, it is necessary for the staff to count inmates on a regular basis. The institution has a system of regularly scheduled and unscheduled counts. There are five (5) official counts during each twenty four (24) hour period. Six on Weekends and Holidays.

OFFICIAL COUNTS

MONDAY THROUGH FRIDAY:
1. Midnight
2. 3:00 A.M.
3. 5:00 A.M.
4. 4:00 P.M. (stand up count)
5. 9:00 P.M.

On Saturdays, Sundays and Holidays there is an additional 10:00 A.M. count.

The following rules will be observed during count time:

1. Inmates must be in their assigned area.
2. 4:00 P.M. and 10:00 A.M. (weekend and holiday) Counts are **stand up counts**. Inmates must be standing next to their bed assignment.
3. There will be **NO MOVING ABOUT OR TALKING** during counts.
4. Staff must see flesh for a proper count, do not cover yourself completely when sleeping.

Detail Census:

1. 7:30 A.M. work days
2. 12:30 P.M. work days

NOTE:
During Detail Census (unofficial counts) you must be at your assigned detail area and make your presence known to your detail supervisor. All unassigned and A&O inmates must be at their assigned unit and make their presence known to the unit officer.

CALL-OUTS:
Are defined as scheduled appointments. A list is posted in each unit every day after 6:00 P.M. for the next working day. It is your responsibility to read and **COMPLY** with any scheduled **CALL-OUT**.

Drug/alcohol Testing:

The Bureau operates a surveillance program that includes random testing, as well as testing of other categories of inmates. Refusal to provide a sample will be considered the same as a positive test, either will result in an incident report.

Loitering/littering:

Inmates are not to loiter around any building entrance area or the Officer's station. DO NOT put hands, feet, or any part of the body on the walls or windows. Disciplinary action will be taken when inmates are caught littering.

TELEPHONE PROCEDURES

Telephones are available for inmate use daily as posted. A thirty minute limit is imposed for each call. Third party calls are strictly prohibited.

ALL INMATE TELEPHONES ARE MONITORED.

Use of an unmonitored telephone for consultation with your attorney may be arranged by contracting your Unit Team.

Inmates may not ordinarily be released from any program assignment for the purpose of making a call. Institutional telephones may not be used without permission of a staff member. The Chaplain can assist inmates with phone calls in cases of a death or serious family emergency.

The Inmate Telephone System-II (ITS-II) is used at FCI Miami. This is a direct dial and collect call system.

You must enter your phone numbers using the TRULINCS computer system. You may input up to thirty (30) active telephone numbers.

NOTE:

800, 900, 976 numbers will not be allowed!

A Personal Access Code (PAC) will be given by Unit Team staff or at the Business Office Open House on Tuesday and Thursday between the hours of 11:00 am and 12:00 noon. Telephone credits can be transferred over the phone lines. Follow instructions as they are given over the phone.

PHONE ACCESS CODE (PAC):

1.   You will be assigned a nine (9) digit Phone Access Code (PAC). The PAC is your confidential code.
2.   The PAC must be used to process all telephone activities.
3.   Distribution of this PAC to other inmates is prohibited.
4.   If you believe your PAC has been compromised, contact your Unit Manager immediately.

TO PLACE A LOCAL CALL:

1.   Listen for the dial tone.
2.   Enter the ten digit telephone number.
3.   Wait for the new dial tone.

4.   Enter your Phone Access Code (PAC).
      Example:(305)555-1234/357926819

TO PLACE A LONG DISTANCE CALL:
1.   Listen for the dial tone.
2.   Enter1, area code and telephone number.
3.   Wait for the new dial tone.
4.   Enter your Phone Access Code (PAC).
      Example: 1-202-555-1234/357926819

TO PLACE AN INTERNATIONAL CALL:
1.   Listen for the dial tone.
2.   Enter 011, country code, city code and telephone number.
3.   Wait for the new dial tone.
4.   Enter your Phone Access Code (PAC).
      Example: 011-35-24-426973/357926819

TO OBTAIN YOUR ITS ACCOUNT BALANCE AND THE COST OF YOUR LAST CALL:

1.   Listen for the dial tone.
2.   Enter 118 and then enter your Phone Access Code (PAC).
      Example: 118/357926819

Additional guidelines have been received at BOP facilities nationwide regarding telephone use.

1.   Only one telephone will be available for use in each housing unit from 7:15 A.M. to 10:30 A.M. and from 12:00 P.M. until the 4:00 P.M. count clears. This telephone is for those on day off, or who work early morning, or late shift hours.

      NOTE: Telephone use may be suspended pending investigation of suspicious telephone conversations (talking in code, making an allusion to criminal activity, etc.).

2.   Inmates will be authorized to place a maximum of 300 minutes of phone calls per month.

3.   The following sanctions will be considered for telephone abuse:

      1st offense: loss of telephone privileges for 6 to 18 months.

      2nd offense: loss of telephone privileges for 16 to 36 months.

      Repetitive violations will be met with increased sanctions.

4.   If you receive an incident report and loss of telephone privileges for abuse of telephones, your Unit team may recommend to the Warden additional telephone restriction pursuant to 28 CFR & 540.100 after the UDC/DHO sanction has expired. This classification could result in you being limited to one telephone call per month. If so classified you will receive written notice from the Warden and instructions on appeals rights.

5. Inmates transferring to Miami, may be subject to the limitation of one telephone call per month, pursuant to 28 CFR & 540.100. Specifically, a criminal conviction involving use of a prison telephone will be scrutinized. Factors such as: recency of the conviction and behavior in prison will also be taken into consideration. If so classified you, will receive written notice from the Warden with instructions on appeal rights.

When using the Inmate Telephone System, you must not engage in the following activities or you will be subject to disciplinary action:

☎   Use the telephone during your work hours without prior authorization of your unit team.

☎   Make a 3-way telephone call.

☎   Make a call that is forwarded to another telephone number, regardless of whether that telephone number is on your approved telephone list.

☎   Discuss or engage in any business related activities over the telephone. Use the telephone to gamble, call gambling hotlines, or discuss gambling odds. Actively trade stocks, commodities, or anything of value or instruct others to do so.

☎   Use the telephone to convey or pass messages from another inmate to a third party.

☎   Make or imply any threat or speak in code to another Person over the telephone.

☎   Use another inmate's PAC number.

☎   Pass the telephone to another inmate or accept the telephone from another inmate after a telephone call has been connected.

☎   Participate in conference calling. Attempt to use the telephone while on telephone restriction.

☎   Use the telephone to contact a volunteer, contract worker, staff member, or any former inmate who is in a halfway house or on supervised release.

☎   Arrange to have anything of value sent to another inmate or inmate's family without staff authorization.

☎   Finally, you must not engage in any other activity or conduct over the telephone which staff interpret as an effort to circumvent our policies and regulations.

UNIT RULES AND REGULATIONS

In order to provide/maintain a safe and sanitary environment for everyone, the following rules will apply to all inmates.

The highest standard of sanitation throughout the institution is expected at all times. You will be held responsible for the condition of your living area.

Respect the rights and property of others. All areas will be ready for inspection at any time between 7:30 A.M. and 4:00 P.M. Monday through Friday, and after 10:00 A.M. on Saturday, Sunday and Holidays. This means; beds will be made properly, areas cleaned, floor, swept and mopped; and trash emptied.

Beds will be neatly made military style. A pillow with a pillow case will be at the head of the bed. A blanket will be on (tucked in) or folded at the foot of the bed. Nothing is to be stored under the mattress. Nothing other than the pillow will be left on top of the bed. Nothing is to be hung or taped to the bed or bed ladder. Shoes only will be lined up evenly and neatly under the bed. No other items are allowed under the bed. Inmates on day off, vacation, or late shift may lie on their bed after it has been made.

Nothing is to be taped, nailed, screwed or glued to walls, doors, or furnishings. Nothing is to be placed on the door window that blocks the full or partial view of the room. Nothing is to be stored on the top of or attached to the locker. No nude or suggestive pictures, calendars, or magazine cut outs will be openly displayed. They must be inside your locker.

Blankets, towels, altered linens or any king of material will not be placed on the floor as rugs. Personal hygiene items will be provided as needed by either the Unit Officer or Unit Staff.

Room assignments changes will be made by Unit Teams Only.

Television Viewing:
The selection of programs to be viewed will be determined by a majority vote of the inmates actually watching T.V. The television designated for sports will have only sports programs. The television designated for general viewing will have only non-sports programs.
Loud talking, yelling, and/or loud noise-making actions will not be tolerated in the T.V. areas. Chairs may be taken to T.V. areas however must be returned to the room when not in use.

NOTE:
There is a weekly sanitation inspection conducted at the Warden's discretion with the Associate Warden, Captain, and Safety Manage. The results of this inspection determines the meal rotation.

Unit Staff will also inspect all areas regularly to include daily room inspections. Randomly, the Unit Manager will conduct official inspections of their unit. The Safety Manager will conduct the required monthly safety and sanitation inspections.

QUIET TIME:

From 9:00 P.M. until 6:00 A.M. (Sunday-Thursday), (9:00 P.M. to 9:00 A.M., weekends and Holidays), all inmates will observe **Quiet Time**. No loud noises (talking, singing, whistling, playing music, card games, etc.) are allowed. **Be considerate of Others.** Smoking is **Prohibited** through out the institution.

VISITING REGULATIONS

Legal visits:

All attorneys must have proper credentials which are, a valid driver's license or identification with a picture and a current bar card. Attorneys or their approved representatives must make prior appointments through the Warden's office to meet with their clients. Legal visits are encouraged during regular visiting days and times (8:00 A.M. to 3:00 P.M., Friday through Mondays). Visitors must be at the processing center before 1:00 P.M. An appointment can be arranged by contacting the Warden's office, 24 hours in advance, by calling (305) 259-2100.

Attorneys with the necessity to review audio or video material concerning the case must contact the Camp Administrator/Executive Assistant this facility to obtain approval to bring the material before coming into the facility. Audio and viewing equipment will be provided.

Social Visits:

The program is based on a **POINT SYSTEM: EVEN & ODD** numbers visiting on separate days. Inmates are identified based on the last digit of the first five numbers of their Register Number. For example, for register number 12389-004, the number 9 will be the identifier number which is an ODD number. All inmates receive six (6) Visiting Point per month.

Weekdays	-	Visits will count as one (1) point.
Weekend and Holidays	-	Visit will count as two (2) points.

NOTE:

During any period of unusual high volume visiting, visits my be limited to 2 hours. Sundays and holidays visiting is a normal high volume visiting day and is subject to 2 hours visits.

NOTE:

Only one group of visitors will be processed for any given inmate for each day. Every visitor is required to provide the Inmate's Last Name, Vehicle Tag Number, Model, Year and Color of car driven to the facility.

Visiting hours are: 8:00 A.M. to 3:00 P.M.. Thursday through Monday. Visitors must be at the processing area (Front Sally Port) by 1:00 P.M. or will not be allowed entrance. The visitors parking lot is open at 7:30 A.M.. All visitors must have a picture identification card in the form of a driver's license, state ID card, or passport. Visitors are permitted to bring a maximum of $25.00 into the visiting room. No credit cards, personal checkbooks, beepers, sun glasses, candies, toys, letters, books, newspapers, makeup, etc.; will be allowed.

Upon commitment, the inmate will submit a list of visitors to his Unit Team. This visiting list will be final upon submission, for ninety (90) days. All changes and/or additions to the visiting list must be submitted as scheduled on a three (3) month basis through your Unit Team. Special visits for other visitors are not encouraged. Special visits must be requested to the Unit Team at least one (1) week in advance. The Unit Manager or his designee has the authority to approve special visits.

The visiting list is limited to eighteen (18) visitors consisting of immediate family members and friends. A Visitors information Questionnaire (BP 309(52) and Authorization for Release Information (Visitor) (BP 310(52) must be completed prior to the approval of any non-immediate family member.
Immediate family members are defined as: parents, step parents and/or foster parents, sisters, brothers, children, and spouse.

Immediate family members with last names different from the inmate's last name, who are not able to verify the relationship through proper documentation, will be treated as non-immediate family members. See your Unit Team for details.

Consular Visits:
When it has been determined that an inmate is a citizen of a foreign country, the Warden must permit the consular representative of that country to visit on matters of legitimate business. Your Unit Team will be able to assist you with phone calls to, or visitation with your consular representative.

Number of Visitors:
Due to space limitation, guidelines are necessary to establish the maximum number of visitors allowed to visit an inmate at one time. During all visitation hours only five adult visitors per inmate will be allowed access to the visiting room. Children small enough to be held at all times, and therefore not requiring a chair, will be the only exception to this policy. A maximum of six visitors are the total allowance for a single visit.

No additional social visitors will be allowed access to the visiting room once a social visit has been initiated. One set of social visitors, up to the maximum allowance, will be allowed access to the visiting room on a single day. At the conclusion of this visit, the inmate's visitation privilege is fulfilled for the single day.

The visiting procedures for Thanksgiving and Christmas Day will be both odd and even with no points being charged for that visiting day. Due to the high volume of expected visits, the visiting period will be limited to a two hour period on a first come/first served basis.

Parents with children (infants) are allowed only the following items: two pampers, one set of clothes, one feeding bottle (milk or juice), a sealed travel packed wipes, and a single layered baby blanket.

All visits will take place in the Visiting Room, located in the Administration Building. Refreshments are sold to make your visits as enjoyable as possible.

Inmates and their visitors are expected to conduct themselves in a quiet and orderly manner. Handshaking, kissing and embracing may take place at the beginning and at the end of the visit only.

Children must be controlled by their parents during the visit. There will be no exchange of packages, letters, or articles in the visiting room. All items brought in the institution by a visitor will be taken back out as he/she departs the facility. The Operation Lieutenant or Staff Duty Officer will consulted prior to denying a visitor's entry into the institution because of the their attire.

Visitor's Dress Code:
The following attire will be prohibited:

- (a) Sleeveless blouses
- (b) Skirts not meeting the knee
- (c) Tight fitting shorts or shorts above the knee
- (d) Absence of undergarments
- (e) See-through clothing
- (f) Halter tops
- (g) Jeans with holes

Inmate's Dress Code:
Inmates will be dressed in khaki trousers and shirts with approved visiting shoes. No tennis shoes will be permitted. Inmates may carry into Visiting Room area the following items:

- (a) One comb
- (b) One handkerchief
- (c) One wedding band (no stone)
- (d) Legal materials (if legal visit only, pre-approved by Unit Team)
- (e) One religious medallion (with chain)

All items taken into the Visiting Room will be inventoried and the same items must leave the Visiting Room. Inmates will be strip searched prior to entering and departing the visiting room. Inmates will not be permitted to carry out any items other than those listed above.

Inmates will not be allowed to bring legal materials into the Visiting Room for legal visits unless previously approved by the Unit Team. This material will be inspected by the Visiting Room Officer for contraband. The contents of legal material will not be read. Legal material may be transferred between the inmate and his visit.

LIST:
Only those visitors who have been authorized will be permitted to visit. Visits will not be permitted for any person(s) who have not been approved before hand.

Upon commitment you may submit a visiting list to your Counselor for approval. Members of the immediate family (wife, children, parents, brothers, sisters) will ordinarily be placed on the approved visiting list automatically.

A common-law spouse will usually be treated as an immediate family member if the common-law relationship has previously been established in a state which recognizes such a status.

All other relations and friends will be required to submit a form authorizing a background investigation before being approved to visit. This form may be obtained from your Counselor. A maximum of eighteen (18) visitors will be authorized on your visiting list.

Children less than 16 years of age must be accompanied by an adult member of the family which is on the approved visiting list.

Adult visitors will not be permitted to leave the visiting room and leave small children in the care of the inmate. Parents are to maintain control of their children at all times.

Visitor Identification:
A driver's license, passport, state identification card, or two other forms of identification with full name and signature will be required. Birth Certificates are not considered proper identification. Visitors will not be permitted entry without proper identification.

A handshake, kiss, or embrace, within reason and good taste, is permitted upon arrival and departure only. The Visiting Room is a public place and children are usually present. You are expected to conduct yourself accordingly.

Visitors are not permitted to bring food into the visiting area. Sandwiches, soft drinks, snacks and candies are available from vending machines in the Visiting Room.

The Federal Correctional Institution is located at 15801 SW 137th Avenue, Miami, Florida 33177, and was dedicated on March 26, 1976 as a facility under the jurisdiction of the United States Department Of Justice, Federal Bureau Of Prisons. The facility is located next to the old Richmond Naval Air Station and the Metro Zoo, just south of the Country Walk Shopping Center, in Southern Dade County, Florida.

WORK ASSIGNMENTS

During the A & O period you will be assigned to various duties by the Unit Officer. Upon completion of A & O program and medical clearance you will be assigned to a work detail. The needs of the institution will be given first consideration when assigning you to a job. Other factors considered in determining your work assignment are, your physical condition, previous work experience, educational level, general attitude, ability to benefit from training, and plans for the future.

JOBS: Examples of jobs available include:
Business Office -   Laundry workers, Commissary workers
Education -   Tutors, Law Clerk, Orderlies
Facilities -   Electric Shop, Landscape, Communication, Plumbing,
                         Painters, and Construction
Food Service -   Cooks, Bakers, Butchers, Salad preparation workers,
                         Dishwashers, Orderlies and Clerks
Health Service -   Medical and Dental Orderlies
Recreation -   Orderlies
Safety -   Clerks
Units -   Orderlies
Unicor -   Cutting, Sewing, Packing, Shipping, Business Office and
                         Quality Assurance
Visiting Room -   Orderlies

Job changes are made by the Unit Manager when there is a justifiable need. Ordinary, you will be on a job 6 months before being considered for a job change. Job changes will be requested by filling out and turning in a Cop-Out to your Counselor. Your request must contain; job being requested, reason for the request, a signature of current supervisor indicating approval, an approval signature of supervisor for job being requested.

Safety devices (goggles, gloves, and safety shoes, etc.). Steel-toed shoes must be worn to work, including positions on the unit.

Inmates must remain on their job assignments during the regular working hours. If there is a reason to leave a work detail, the supervisor must be notified immediately. All inmates are responsible for checking the call-out and change sheet daily. Missing a call-out could result in receiving an incident report. Detail supervisors must be notified of an inmate's call-out.

Performance Pay:
If you are assigned to a paid work assignment (not including UNICOR), you will be awarded a Performance Pay if your Work Supervisor recommends you for it.

Presently, pay rates are as follows:
Grade 4	$0.12/hr.
Grade 3	$0.17/hr.
Grade 2	$0.29/hr.
Grade 1	$0.40/hr.
Maintenance Pay	$5.25/month

These rates are subject to change according to Federal Bureau of Prisons Policy. You may receive Performance Pay for a maximum of seven (7) hours per work day, and a maximum of thirty-five (35) hours per week. You will be paid only for the number of hours you worked in a satisfactory manner. Each work detail has a specific number of positions allotted which are utilized to receive performance pay. If you are in FRP (Financial Responsibility Program) Refuse status, you cannot earn above Maintenance Pay.

If you are having a problem concerning your job pay, you should report these problems immediately to your Detail Supervisor.

Job payments are deposited in your Commissary account no later than the twenty-ninth of the month.

FEDERAL PRISON INDUSTRIES UNICOR

Federal Prison Industries (UNICOR) is a self sustained, government owned, corporation that was established by an act of Congress in 1934. All products manufactured by UNICOR are sold only to government agencies, i.e., Veterans Affairs, Department of Defense, GSA, Armed Forces and Justice Department, including the Bureau of Prisons. UNICOR's primary objective is to train and employ inmates confined within the Bureau of Prisons. Long term studies have shown that participation in UNICOR work program provide skills and work ethics that will enhance the probability of inmates not returning to prison upon release.

Here at FCI-Miami, the UNICOR operation consists of a Textile Cut & Sew Factory which manufactures jackets and linens. The factory employs approximately 280 inmates within it's Cutting, Sewing, Folding, Packing, Shipping, Business Office and Quality Assurance departments. Any inmate is eligible to work in UNICOR providing he has completing the medical and educational requirements. The factory hires handicapped inmates when positions are available.

All individuals interested in obtaining a work assignment in UNICOR may submit an Inmate Request to Staff Member (COPOUT) to the factory Manager who will place names on a waiting list. Inmates with prior UNICOR experience will be given priority in hiring. Their names will be placed in the top 10% of the waiting list. Inmates participating in the Inmate Financial Responsibility Program having fines of over $2,000.00 will also be placed on the priority list.

Starting pay is $.23 cents per hour (grade 5) based on a 7 1/2 hour work day, which begins at 7:20 A.M. and ends at 3:35 P.M., and may progress to grade 1 which is $1.15 per hour. Promotions are based on positions available, production, job performance, and general attitude, i.e. cooperation with supervisors, adherence to the dress codes and rules within UNICOR as well as those of the institution. All inmate workers must comply with safety and sanitation policies and regulations. In addition, promotions in UNICOR are contingent upon educational requirements that must be achieved by the inmate.

<u>CONCLUSION</u>

Hopefully this information will assist you in your first days in federal custody and/or the Federal Correctional Institution Miami. This booklet is intended to be a guide. Changes in procedures may occur that effect procedures outlined in this booklet. Every effort will be made to inform the inmate population of these changes, any significant changes will be posted on your Unit Bulletin Board. Changes will not be made to this booklet until reprint. Feel free to ask any staff member for assistance, particularly your unit team (Counselors, Case Managers and Unit Manager).